SPANISH BUREAUCRATIC-PATRIMONIALISM IN AMERICA

Spanish Bureaucratic-Patrimonialism In America

MAGALI SARFATTI

Foreword by
DAVID E. APTER

Price—$1.75

Institute of International Studies
University of California, Berkeley

©, 1966, BY THE REGENTS OF THE UNIVERSITY OF CALIFORNIA

FOREWORD

Even a quick glance at the roster of developing nations shows such differences in political structure and style that it seems an impossible task to compare them in any meaningful way. This situation, although it presents great difficulties, is not altogether hopeless. A number of scholars have recently attempted to create general categories which allow the comparison of widely different systems. One effort, a pioneering one, involving the joint efforts of several area specialists, undertook the examination of five main geographic areas of the world; the intra-regional comparisons led to inter-regional ones. [Louis Hartz, The Founding of New Societies (New York: Harcourt, Brace & World, 1964).] There have been many other attempts, of course. Some of the most brilliant theoretical work leading to propositions about social change was begun in the latter nineteenth and early twentieth centuries by such historical sociologists as Coulanges, Durkheim, Weber, and others, who dealt specifically with the role of religion, the city, and the structure of primitive and modern society. Their efforts to elicit different sets of norms, structures, and appropriate forms of behavior germane to "traditional" as compared with "modern" society has left us with a body of important insights, the significance of which is still being tested. In particular, Max Weber's comparison of complex traditional political systems with modern ones, focussing on the problem of "legitimacy," not only opens up a range of interesting questions about the comparison of traditional types of authority with modern ones, but also makes possible the comparison of traditional systems in order to reveal their differences. This seems essential before going on to more contemporary studies.

Such interest in the traditional setting continues to grow. Some scholars would have it that the pattern of development first established by a particular traditional system sustains itself long after the traditional system has, overtly at least, disappeared. Certain norms may continue, preventing new and modern forms of political structure from functioning usefully. Patterns of behavior germane to the traditional setting may continue well into the modern period, confounding it and preventing it from developing. Some political historians, who regard the colonial form of traditionalism as an inheritance which cannot be escaped in modern times, see these patterns as critical fragments of the European tradition continuing to unfold in almost an Hegelian sense. Where the colonial experience has involved a significant cluster of European settlement ("a fragment of European culture," as Hartz calls it), not only does the European culture continue to survive, but it is transformed into a new nationalism. As Hartz says:

Feudalism comes back at us as the French-Canadian Spirit, liberalism as the American Way of Life, radicalism as the Australian Legend. But even this is not all. The European ideology, buried and refurbished, is extended to African and Indian relationships which in Europe it did not have, so that it inspires a series of racial formulations apparently outside its compass. Suarez lies hidden beneath the Latin-American encomienda, Calvin beneath the slavery of Dutch South Africa. [Op. cit., p. 5.]

Hartz goes on to say that the traditional element remains particularly strong where "feudalism" develops, and he applies this term to Latin America. Whether or not the term is appropriate, it is certainly the case that certain characteristics of traditional Spanish bureaucratic practice have had an amazing durability, particularly in the old centers of Spanish rule, such as Lima. It is therefore of particular interest to raise some of the questions pertaining to the "legitimacy" of that traditional system which first were enunciated by the historical sociologists, and to the normative bases of authority (particularly the relationship of these to Catholicism), in order to understand what came later, and to see the relevance of traditional "survivals."

This study by Miss Magali Sarfatti is an effort to articulate some of the main characteristics of the Spanish bureaucratic-patrimonial system. Using a generalized Weberian model of patrimonial authority, she has examined the interrelationships between normative and structural, religious and political, and theoretical and empirical aspects of the Spanish traditional system.

This monograph represents the first in a series of studies of the Political Modernization Project of the Institute of International Studies, University of California, Berkeley. Subsequent essays will deal with the new forms of society which have developed in Latin America, particularly in Argentina, Peru, and Chile, leading to analysis of the contemporary scene and of the politics of industrialization. Members of this project are working on the following: the role of Spanish traditionalism (Miss Sarfatti), the role of the military in relation to professionalism (Mrs. Liisa North), the formation of political movements and parties (Mr. José Nun), the relationships between political entrepreneurs and technicians (Professor David E. Apter and Miss Sarfatti), and the pattern of industrial development (Miss Alcira Leiserson).

Each of the monographs will serve as a working paper for more systematic comparisons between the three countries under discussion, and, as well, prepare the ground for broader studies comparing them with West African countries in the early stages of their modernization.

David E. Apter

ACKNOWLEDGMENTS

I wish to express my thanks to Dr. David Apter, Director of the Politics of Modernization Project, for his guidance throughout the preparation of this paper. He spurred me to undertake this exploration into the colonial structure of Spanish America, a task perhaps beyond my capacities.

From many of my colleagues, and in particular Mrs. Liisa North and Miss Arlene Eisen, I received friendly cooperation and invaluable advice. I should make special mention of the enlightening comments and patience of José Nun, Visiting Lecturer at the Department of Political Science at Berkeley, and of the innumerable discussions in which he provided help and encouragement.

I also want to thank Professor Richard Herr of the Department of History at Berkeley for his general comments and, in particular, for his criticism of the sections dealing with Spain. I am much indebted to Professor Aaron Cicourel, Department of Sociology at Santa Barbara, for having read the first version of this manuscript, and helping with the necessary revision of the basic outline.

I wish to thank in particular Mr. Paul Gilchrist, Editor for the Institute of International Studies, for his great patience in dealing with my unorthodox English, and for giving to the text whatever rigor of expression it may have. To Mrs. Gloria Mims, Mrs. Beatrice Tallent, and Miss Kathy Goldman, who typed the various versions of this paper, I owe my apologies and my gratitude.

Magali Sarfatti

TABLE OF CONTENTS

	FOREWORD David E. Apter	v
	INTRODUCTION	1
I.	THE STRUCTURAL AND NORMATIVE CHARACTERISTICS OF SPANISH BUREAUCRATIC-PATRIMONIALISM	5
II.	THE IMPERIAL BUREAUCRACY IN AMERICA: ORGANIZATION AND PRACTICE	21
III.	SPANISH BUREAUCRATIC-PATRIMONIALISM AND COLONIAL SOCIETY	38
IV.	PATTERNS OF URBANIZATION AND URBAN ATTITUDES: THE BREAKDOWNS OF THE MODEL	64
V.	THE REVOLUTIONARY CHALLENGE	93
	APPENDIX: THE INDIANS IN COLONIAL SPANISH AMERICA Arlene Eisen	101
	GLOSSARY OF SPANISH TERMS	125

LIST OF DIAGRAMS

DIAGRAM OF THE ORGANIZATION OF THE SPANISH COLONIAL
BUREAUCRACY   Facing 22

RELATIONS BETWEEN ECCLESIASTICAL AND LAY HIERARCHIES
IN THE SPANISH COLONIAL SYSTEM   23

DIAGRAM OF THE JUDICIARY IN THE SPANISH COLONIAL SYSTEM   24

INTRODUCTION

A rich historical literature dealing with the Spanish imperial system is increasingly available for review by political scientists and sociologists interested in modern Latin America. So richly textured a system, with its capacity to appear again and again through history in various guises, remains a puzzle, if only because of its durability and persistence. It is often the case that patterns of contemporary behavior in Latin America are products, many times translated, of durable proprieties, commitments, and responsibilities which had their source in an almost medieval concept of the organic community. The principle of the community was expressed through a sacred and mystical order, while its practice was in war, conquest, and evangelizing.

Any attempt to fit so complex a subject into a schematic pattern naturally does violence to this richness. Nevertheless, we shall rend complex events from their historical context in order to rearrange them for analytical purposes, a necessary first step in the attempt to assess the present consequences of Spanish bureaucratic-patrimonialism.

It is the need to relate the past to the present which alone justifies this selective and overly schematic view of the socio-political framework that was common to Spanish America before Independence. Our purpose is to reach a tentative sociological assessment of both the colonial society and the independence movements. By this means we will help to explain the persistence of certain characteristics and relationships throughout the formative years of some of the "old-new nations" of Latin America. Although such an incomplete and tentative essay in historical sociology can shed little light on the problems of contemporary societies, for comparative purposes it can be useful to delve into what is generally assumed to be the "traditional" structure which today's developing nations have to overcome.

The Spanish colonial system was the first comprehensive expression of European expansionism. The tasks faced by Spain were formidable: territorial occupation on a yet unseen scale; the submission and organization of peoples of different origins and different cultures, and their conversion to Christianity; the implantation of a colonial economy that would make the conquest profitable for the Spanish monarchy; the organization of the existing labor force; and the institutional and political organization of the new kingdoms attached to the Castilian crown in a manner that would ensure the king's supremacy over the social

SPANISH BUREAUCRATIC-PATRIMONIALISM IN AMERICA

forces of the remote colonies to a degree unknown in Spain itself. The measures employed to accomplish these tasks coalesced in a system which was, on the whole, remarkably coherent. We shall analyze here the main characteristics of the Spanish patrimonial bureaucracy in its normative and structural aspects. By structural aspects we mean the particular political organizations developed by the Spaniards for their overseas territories. They embodied a particular conception of authority which is closely related to the Weberian patrimonial model. Accordingly, we shall briefly delineate the key characteristics of this model before analyzing its application in the Spanish American case. The normative aspects--that is, here, the ideologic constellation in which political conceptions were rooted--were expressed in a formal body of doctrine which was intimately wedded with the socio-political conditions of the time. It was a neo-scholastic version of the classic Thomist conceptions, which both reflected the realities of monarchic authority in sixteenth century Spain and gave strong doctrinal basis for its implantation and expansion in the New World.

Before starting our analysis, however, we must give some consideration to the legitimacy of translating into a model a complex historical system which emerged after years of adjustment and evolution. The nature of cultural contact in a situation of conquest is particularly relevant to this discussion.

It has been argued by an eminent anthropologist--George M. Foster--that the the simple theory of acculturation is inadequate to deal with the composite cultures resulting from "colonization."[1] In the classic approach, such cultures would be synthetic, the accommodated result of the contact between the "donor" and the "recipient" cultures. The problem of explaining the mechanisms involved and the reasons for the selection and predominance of certain cultural traits arises immediately, and is unsatisfactorily solved by either functional explanations or the theory of "proportional representation" (the predominant "imported" traits are those most frequently present in the "contact" situation). Foster proposes to use an intermediate concept, that of "conquest culture," which presupposes "that the government. . . of the donor culture has some degree of military and political control over the recipient people, and that this control is utilized to bring about planned changes in the way of life of this group."[2] In other words, conquest implies that force and violence may accompany and even aid the transmission of certain cultural characteristics. On the other hand, distance from the mother country and

---

[1] Culture and Conquest (Chicago: Quadrangle Books, 1960).

[2] Ibid., p. 11.

INTRODUCTION

the purpose of conquest imposes a selection at the outset, at least among the artifacts and techniques to be exported.

In the Spanish American case, although the Spaniards from various provinces were not proportionately represented among the first conquerors and emigrants, the conquest brought together enterprising people from several different regional "subcultures"; thus, an amalgamated form of the diverse and fragmentary culture of the mother country was brought to America. To this "conquest culture," defined by Foster as "the result of processes that screen the more dynamic, expanding culture, winnowing out and discarding a high percentage of all traits, complexes and configurations found in it, and determining new contexts and combinations for export,"[3] the conquerors themselves were exposed for the first time.

According to Foster, there are both "formal" and "informal" screening processes that occur in the donor culture before the recipient culture effects a second screening. (All of Foster's anthropological work in Spain is devoted to the assessment of the _informal_ process of reduction.) The historical characteristics of the Spanish conquest--the early centralization of the tasks of colonization and the deliberate standardization of the "exported" institutions--explain the _formal_ screening. "It is clear," writes Foster, "that the formally transmitted categories of culture, in which Church and State policy were predominant, are Castilian, rather than Andalusian-Extremaduran."[4] (The latter were predominant among the cultural traits transmitted through _informal_ channels.) Thus, for instance, the version of Catholicism brought to America by the evangelizers was expurgated of its Spanish folk elements. Bureaucracy, as we shall see, was centrally constructed around principles which, in Spain itself, had to reckon with existing social forces, while for America "it was possible to draw up . . . what the rulers thought to be an ideal Spanish political and economic system, one which could disregard the rights and privileges acquired over the years in Spain by individual cities or groups, or social classes."[5] In other words, a deliberate policy of the Crown introduced in the newfound lands some features that were only imperfectly realized in Spain. These features tended to coalesce into a "model." In spite of the diversity of situations resulting from the conquest, one is justified in speaking of Spanish America as a complex with some homogeneous characteristics, "since one of the two usual variables in acculturation

---

[3]Ibid., p. 12.

[4]Ibid., p. 231.

[5]Ibid., pp. 15-16.

settings, the donor culture, was relatively standardized."[6]

We shall deal first with the "ideal pattern" that the Crown abstracted from the Spanish context and imposed upon its overseas provinces. As we study its application, the contradictions implicit in the model, and the further contradictions engendered by its actual functioning, will lead us to an analysis of colonial society from the point of view of its articulations within the structures of government. From this, we shall try to pave the way for an understanding of the independence movements. Some themes to be specifically stressed include: (1) the social conflicts arising from the "subordination" of the Creole elites and the position of the Indians in colonial society (this last topic will be discussed in an appendix presenting some information relevant to an understanding of the role of the "rural masses" in the independence movements and of caste and race lines in the colonial society), and (2) the importance of the urban nuclei in the Spanish American territories. A brief outline of the origins of the secession from Spain will introduce some final considerations. In these, we shall try to sketch an approach to the analysis of social action after the Spanish system of government had been replaced by the "new" political structures in the first years of attempted unification and nation-building.

---

[6]Ibid., p. 17.

I

THE STRUCTURAL AND NORMATIVE CHARACTERISTICS OF SPANISH BUREAUCRATIC-PATRIMONIALISM

When Columbus was seeking royal patronage and financial support for his enterprise, Spain was already well advanced along the road to unification under a single absolute monarchy, though historians insist upon the differences between the kingdoms of Castile and Aragon and, as well, between the personalities and policies of Isabella and Ferdinand. As C. H. Haring points out, if the stable government of Aragon, with its traditional corporate liberties (the *fueros*)* and the well-established authority of the *Cortes*, was "severely left alone" by the new sovereigns, Castile was reorganized under the unquestioned supremacy of the Crown. In Haring's words:

> In so doing, [the kings] laid the foundations of a royal absolutism which ultimately extended over the whole of Spain. . . . They were also unwittingly releasing the energies of Castile for the work of conquest and settlement overseas; and the institutions they created and developed in Castile were soon to be transferred to America and to prevail there for three hundred years.[1]

Thus, as was said before, a "purified" model--abstracted, mainly, from the context of the central kingdoms of Spain--shaped the policy of the Crown in the territories of America throughout the sixteenth century. This was not only because these territories were dynastically attached to Castile, as direct and exclusive possessions of the Crown, but also because the peoples of central and southwestern Spain were privileged with regard to the possibilities of emigration, and thus predominant in number. It has been suggested, furthermore, in relation to a very important feature--the pattern of municipal settlement--that "the pattern of Spanish New World conquest obeyed forces and circumstances analogous to those of the peninsular Reconquest."[2]

---

*See Glossary of Spanish Terms, pp. 125-29.

[1] *The Spanish Empire in America* (New York: Harcourt, Brace & World, Inc., 1963), pp. 2-3. On this point, see also R. Trevor-Davies, *The Golden Century of Spain* (London: Macmillan, 1961).

[2] R. Morse, "Urbanization in Latin America," *Latin American Re-*

SPANISH BUREAUCRATIC-PATRIMONIALISM IN AMERICA

The wars of reconquest helped to curb feudal power and aided in the development of the Spanish national monarchy. The fluidity brought about by the advancing frontier, the central role of towns, and the necessity of centralized leadership derived from the situation of "permanent" war and prevented the crystallization of "classical feudalism." The reconquest provided the Crown of Castile with new lands and prebends that could be distributed among its auxiliaries and used to transform the feudal barons into a dependent noblesse de cour. The emergence of large strata of emancipated peasants in the reconquered territories, the privileges gained or preserved by the urban bourgeoisies, and--among other factors not directly linked with the war--the power of the Mesta, or corporation of sheep raisers, reinforced this process. Thus, not even in the sphere of economic organization did the manorial pattern prevail in Spain. War required Castile to organize its finances, industry, and trade--not to speak of the discipline it imposed upon the Christian armies--for national objects, on a national basis. Such a pattern of development continued despite the financial and economic consequences of the expulsion of the Moors and the Jews in the fifteenth and sixteenth centuries.

Thus, the Crown of Castile, through its leadership in the holy wars, gained direct control of an army, a treasury, and vast territories that it bestowed, without threatening its supremacy, upon its deserving subjects. The Inquisition, as a sometimes too powerful ally, also acted as a strong buttress of royal power. In comparison with the rest of Europe, then, the bases for the emergence of a strong central state were laid relatively early in Spain: "The ties between all subjects and the state were never displaced by personal ties between vassals and lord."[3] Thus, at the outset, the first colonizing nation of Europe embodied a political conception the content of which was both modern (being part of the rise of national states in Western Europe) and traditional (deriving its patrimonial structure from the medieval body of political thought). Its patrimonial structure was particularly visible in the Spanish American context. However, before going on to a discussion of patrimonialism in Spain and its empire, we shall present a description of patrimonial power borrowed from Weber.

---

search Review, I, 1, Fall 1965, p. 37.

[3] See the arguments of the historian of medieval Spain, C. Sánchez Albornoz, presented by R. Morse in "The Heritage of Latin America," in Louis Hartz, ed., The Founding of New Societies (New York: Harcourt, Brace & World, 1964), pp. 144-46, as well as Morse's own views on Latin America, pp. 147-51.

THE STRUCTURAL AND NORMATIVE CHARACTERISTICS

THE STRUCTURE OF THE PATRIMONIAL STATE

Patrimonial power is, for Weber, one of the main types of authority legitimized by tradition. It grows out of the narrow sphere of domestic power (that is, generally, land-based lordship) by an extension of the patriarchal bonds that linked the lord to his kin, retainers, and serfs. "The attainment of a 'political' power, that is the power of a domestic lord over other patriarchs not subjected to his domestic power, implies the existence, within the sphere of domestic power, of power relations that are different in degree and content, but not in structure [from the patriarchal-domestic ones]."[4] In effect, patrimonial power tends "to subject in absolute ways to the power of the lord the extra-patrimonial political subjects, as well as the patrimonial subjects, and to consider all relations of power as a personal possession of the lord, corresponding to his domestic power and possessions." Patrimonial power strives to extend that authority grounded on the respect for tradition (also binding for the lord himself) and on the respect for the person of the lord. By so doing, the successful patrimonial lord links himself to those he dominates "by a community of consent . . . supported by the belief that the traditional exercise of seignorial power is the legitimate right of the lord." In this sense, tradition limits the arbitrariness of the lord, even in the patriarchal domestic sphere: "[O]mnipotent with regard to a single dependent, . . . he is impotent in front of the totality of his dependents."

However, the extension of "indirect" domination depends objectively on the control (ideally aiming at a monopoly) by the lord of the two powers that are specifically "political"--namely, military and judicial power. The availability of a military force, independent from the subjects but directly dependent upon the lord, is essential to the establishment of patrimonial power. Similarly, the existence of a body of administrative officers enjoying the absolute confidence of the lord and as subordinate as possible to his power is necessary to the effectiveness of his rule. In both cases, the "good will" of these necessary auxiliaries depends on the rewards they receive; hence, for the prince,

---

[4]Unless otherwise indicated, all the quotations in the following discussion of Weber are from *Wirtschaft und Gesellschaft*. We have used here the Italian translation [Max Weber, *Economia e Società*, Pietro Rossi, ed. (Milano: Edizioni di Comunità, 1961)]. The parts relied upon most heavily are the following: Vol. II, Chap. IX: "The Sociology of Power," in particular, Sections IV ("Patriarchal and Patrimonial Power"), V (Feudalism, Status Groups and Patrimonialism") and IX ("The Rational Institution of State, Political Parties and Modern Parliaments--Sociology of the State"). The English translations used herein are mine.

SPANISH BUREAUCRATIC-PATRIMONIALISM IN AMERICA

the paramount importance of a treasury under his sole and complete control. (While presupposing land-based lordship, the development of patrimonial power is thus often conditioned by the existence of commercial profits; hence the importance of commercial monopolies.) The necessary rationalization of finances, brought about by increases of seignorial revenues, leads patrimonialism along the way to "a rational bureaucratic administration, with a regulated system of money taxes."

This brief analysis of the genesis of patrimonial power and of its more distinctive traits suggests the sources of its weakness and the threats it will have to overcome. In the first place, there is an excessive dependence on the patrimonial armies --the main danger for the military monarchies analyzed by Weber. Secondly (an element more relevant to our discussion), there is the emergence of a status group of functionaries (Stand) entrenched in their privileges. "Any separation of the functionaries from the intimate community [of the lord's retainers] naturally implies the loosening of the immediate power of the lordship." The benefices granted by the prince (whether assigned benefices in nature, fiefs, or revenues) result in a tendency toward the appropriation of their offices by the body of patrimonial bureaucrats. In Weber's words: "Any prebendal decentralization of the bureaucratic administration, any delimitation of competence determined by the division of the potential revenues between the competitive functionaries, any appropriation of benefices, implies, in the patrimonial state, not a rationalization, but a stereotypization."

If the prince has sufficient power, the tendency toward the constitution of a Stand (accentuated by the sale of offices) will be countervailed by his arbitrariness, that is, by his power to revoke or rescind at will all privileges and appropriations. The arbitrary type of patrimonialism can reach, thus, some degree of "separation between problems of office and private problems, between the patrimony of office and private patrimony, and delimit the power of the functionaries." Bureaucratic recruitment and advances are based on personal confidence and not on objective qualifications; they reflect the more or less precarious balance reached by the prince in his effort to create and maintain a bureaucracy completely dependent upon his power. In each case, the position of the patrimonial bureaucrat must remain what it originally was--"an emanation of his relation of purely personal submission to the lord," of which his own power over the lord's subjects is but an external aspect.

In this situation, regulated by stereotypes rather than by rational rules, a threat to patrimonial power comes from the de facto use that the functionaries make of the power vested in them. Consuetudinary practices modifying the lord's original decrees--which are particularly bound to arise when the lord's agents are in remote provinces, out of his direct and immediate

THE STRUCTURAL AND NORMATIVE CHARACTERISTICS

sphere of power--appear in the wake of any weakness of the central power, and contribute to its deterioration.

These considerations explain the typical structure of patrimonial bureaucracies. To protect the indivisibility of his power, the prince seeks various guarantees. Periodic visits to his territories (either by the prince in person or by his <u>missi dominici</u>), the requirement of periodic visits by his agents to the Court, the short duration of terms of office, "the exclusion of functionaries from regions where they own land or have kinship ties," the creation of overlapping administrative powers in the same district, and the division of competences among local functionaries are among the most important.

If the prince is successful in controlling the patrimonial bureaucracy, he will have a strong weapon in his "continuous struggle against the various centrifugal local powers." Among these, the most threatening are the local lords of the land, who tend in the first place toward autonomy, i.e., they tend to act as intermediates between the prince and his subjects: "They demand first of all and above all that the patrimonial prince respect, or directly guarantee, their own patrimonial power over their subordinates. . . . If the stratum of independent notables has to be completely displaced, [the prince] must have his own means of administrative organization, in order to establish, among the local populations, an authority roughly equivalent to that of the displaced notables."

Historically, the patrimonial princes sought to bolster their power by the foundation of cities (thus subjecting the lords of the land to a local administrative apparatus), or by using a church universalized and politicized by the state as a support. (The latter method failed in the case of the Eastern Roman Empire, and, later, the German emperors felt that the creation by the popes of a purely ecclesiastical bureaucracy threatened their own specific means of domination over the local powers.) Whatever the specific means employed, the patrimonial prince tries to oppose the encroachments attempted on his power by the feudal lords by using a group of non-propertied functionaries against them; in some cases (as in the very particular case of the English justices of the peace) he will win to his side a group of minor local notables, entrust to them (in semi-autonomous fashion) the administrative functions, and play them against the landed barons.

However, the typical way of life and mentality of these notables are more closely related to feudal concepts than to the concepts underlying a patrimonial bureaucracy. In the latter, "the functionary derives his dignity not from his 'being,' but from his 'functions,' expecting to gain from his service advantages and a career." His formal training (be it "literary-intellectual," as in China, or juridical, as in the European

SPANISH BUREAUCRATIC-PATRIMONIALISM IN AMERICA

monarchies) is often based upon this principle. (Where the state has not developed its own system of education, and where some affinities exist between the aims of the patrimonial state and the dominant religious ethic, "the religious organization takes education in its hands.") It is true that the feudal stress on the personal reverence of the lord makes of the bond between lord and vassal--although it is extra-patrimonial--an extreme case of patrimonialism. However, "feudalism represents the power of the few, of those who are apt to bear arms," while patriarchial patrimonialism is founded on "the domination of the masses by a single individual." The ideal relation tends here toward the authoritarian relationship between fathers and sons; a paternalistic disposition is inherent in the patrimonial state, where the ideal is not "the hero," but "the father of the land." Thus, when the Stand autonomy of the feudal nobles and the economic autonomy of the bourgeoisie have been successfully checked by the patrimonial prince, his power can be geared toward the enforcement of a "social policy" aimed "at ensuring the benevolence of the masses." The main characteristics of the patrimonial structure of power analyzed by Weber can be briefly summed up in a simple diagram:

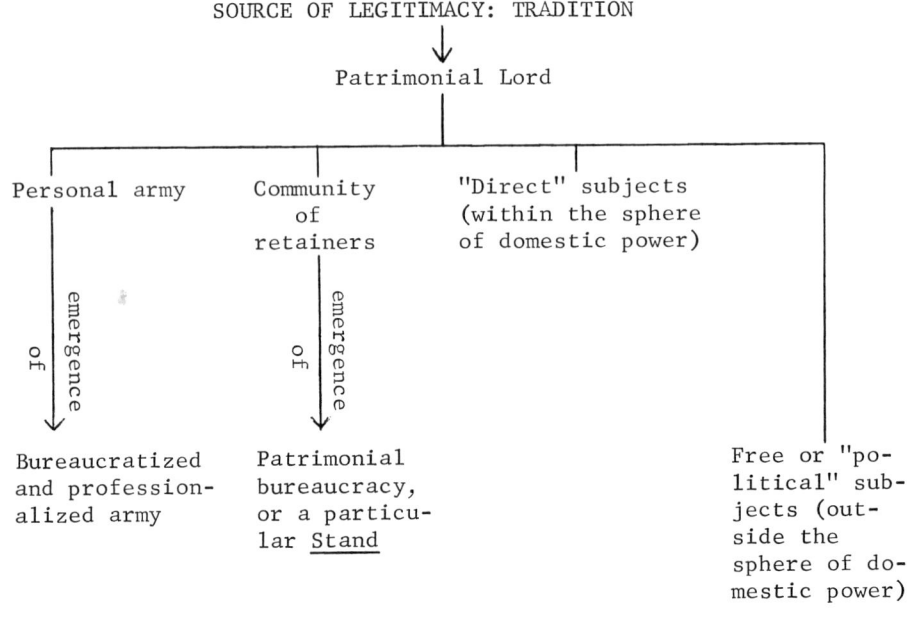

THE STRUCTURAL AND NORMATIVE CHARACTERISTICS

THE NORMATIVE BASIS OF SPANISH PATRIMONIALISM: THE THOMISTIC MODEL

For Weber, the subjects of the patrimonial lord vest in him, by the force of tradition, a legitimate right to govern. Tradition, at the same time, whether diffuse or embodied in a set of explicit principles, defines the rightful expectations of the subjects and thus the limits of the lord's will.

In the Spanish case, the rise of the Castilian monarchy was legitimized from the very beginning by its role as soldier and guardian of the Catholic faith. A particular interpretation of the Catholic medieval tradition given in the sixteenth century by the neo-scholastic thinkers of the Counter-Reformation--Francisco de Vitoria (c. 1483-1546) and, in particular, Francisco Suarez (1548-1617)--is generally regarded as the formalized ideological basis of the Hapsburgs' patrimonial absolutism. Indeed, neo-scholasticism offered, in the words of R. Morse, a "sophisticated theoretical formulation of the ideals and many sociological realities of the Spanish patrimonial state."[5] On the other hand, it can be maintained that "it was the vigorous imposition of these ideas by the state that assured their indisputable primacy. The State found the basis it needed for strengthening its autocracy de jure in the doctrines of the Counter-Reformation; joining these doctrines with the will to absolutism gave royal authority invincible power."[6]

The system imposed upon the Indies by the Spanish government is characterized by R. Morse, in an early article, as "a dominant Thomistic order, with recessive Machiavellian traits."[7] And, in effect, as he has suggested later, the Thomistic philosophy revived in the age of Spain's Barockscholastik "was more relevant to XVIth century Spain and her overseas empire than to feudal XIIIth century Europe, in which it was conceived."[8] Aquinas' ideal system applied more to urban than to rural societies. In the words of Ernst Troeltsch, "Catholic theory [was] comparatively independent of feudal tenure and the feudal system."[9]

---

[5] "The Heritage . . .," p. 155.

[6] José Luis Romero, A History of Argentine Political Thought, trans. by Thomas McGann (Stanford University Press, 1963), p. 15.

[7] "Toward a Theory of Spanish American Government," reprinted from The Journal of the History of Ideas, XV, 1954, under the title "Political Theory and the Caudillo" in Hugh H. Hamill, ed., Dictatorship in Spanish America (New York: A. Knopf, 1965).

[8] "The Heritage . . .," esp. pp. 153-57.

[9] The Social Teachings of the Christian Churches (New York, 1960), I, p. 314.

SPANISH BUREAUCRATIC-PATRIMONIALISM IN AMERICA

We shall briefly outline here the Thomist principles which inspired the Suarezian doctrine, as well as the elements stressed by neo-scholastic thought. In so doing, we shall try to link the ideological premises of Spanish patrimonialism to the relations between tradition and patrimonial power indicated by Weber.

Medieval political thought centered upon the search for a definition of the power of the Church--its structure, basis, and legitimacy. The resulting concept of the Church, according to Sheldon Wolin, emerged from reflection over its double identity-- that is a mystical unity whose secular role made it the governing organ of Christendom.[10] This synthesis, as we shall see, bears some resemblance to modern political societies. Wolin describes the medieval representation of the Church as a "somewhat confusing image of an imperial power which also professed to be a community." Accordingly, the struggle of empires and national monarchies against the papacy can best be understood as a conflict between two orders of government (phrased in terms borrowed from the papal writers). "It was a situation," says Wolin, "where one political theory, which often frantically sought to bolster its cause by borrowing religious ideas from its opponents, was pitted against another political theory which spoke in the name of an organized religion that had become deeply politicized in thought and structure."

The arguments establishing the superiority of the pope over temporal rulers were powerfully and clearly elaborated in Aquinas' Summa Theologiae. The connection he established between the communal foundation of the Church, grounded in the sacraments, and the element of power, stresses at once the mystical unity of the society of believers and the unity of the corpus subordinated to its directing head. The effects of this political-religious theory on the Western tradition in general and, in particular, on the political conceptions upheld by imperial Spain, can be found in Aquinas' conception of the sacrament of Order. The notion of "order" was "the primary medium through which the 'political' was diffused throughout the Thomistic system," and the sacrament itself was "the grand remedy against 'divisions in the community.' . . . [The sacrament] therefore required power, and order within the Church was concerned with the various gradations of power." Church and Creation were similarly organized along hierarchical lines which established the distinctive identity of the parts by linking them to the whole. Hierarchy was then the articulate

---

[10]Political Vision (Boston: Little, Brown & Co., 1960). We shall follow closely in this and the following paragraphs Wolin's discussion of medieval Christian thought. Unless otherwise indicated, the quotations as well as the general ideas presented are taken from Chap. IV, in particular pp. 131-40.

expression of unity, and this unity derived from the subordination to the center, the "prime mover who imparted a regular and purposeful motion to the whole." In St. Thomas' words: "One hierarchy is one principality--that is, one multitude ordered in one way under the government of one ruler. Now such a multitude would not be ordered, but confused, if there were not in it different orders. So the nature of a hierarchy requires diversity of orders."[11] And,

> Wherever there are movers ordained to one another, the power of the second mover must needs be derived from the power of the first mover, since the second mover does not move except insofar as it is moved by the first. Therefore we observe the same in all those who govern, namely, that the plan of government is derived by the secondary governors from the governor in chief. Thus the plan of what is to be done in a state flows from the King's command to his inferior administrators.[12]

We can now sketch more abstractly the principles of Thomist thought relevant to our discussion. Both the static and the dynamic aspects of power converge in a single center. "Movement" derives from this center, which imparts life and purpose to the whole. The articulations of hierarchy reflect, so to speak, the ways in which each part serves the overall purpose of the body. A non-rational "oneness" derives from communion with the supraordinate principle, the articulations of hierarchy being the skeleton, the "material" support of the whole. The power delegated by the center to the parts cannot be measured by rational criteria of means-end adjustment, but reflects, rather, the greater or lesser distance from the "prime mover."

If we grant that, in a world that has not yet experienced "disenchantment," religion represents one fundamental form of belief "in the inviolability of what has always existed," we can consider the "eternal law"--the "law of God"--as representing tradition in a Weberian sense. In his reflection on the structure of the Church, which embodied the "eternal law," Aquinas was in a certain sense seeking the model for all other structures of power, since these were ultimately sanctioned by God's vicars. Human societies had to be matched with the structured harmony of the universe. Socio-political hierarchies being a part of the greater hierarchical order of Creation, the temporal ruler is responsible to God, or His representative, for the preservation of Christian justice. Casuistry, as an interpretation of the natural order,

---

[11]*Summa Theologiae*, Pegis edition, I, Q.108, Art. 2.

[12]*Ibid.*, Ia, IIae, Q.93, Art. 3.

SPANISH BUREAUCRATIC-PATRIMONIALISM IN AMERICA

becomes more important than human law, because to adjudicate is to determine whether a given case affects all of society or whether it can be dispatched by an ad hoc decision. . . . The supreme power . . . must enjoy full legitimacy to serve as the ultimate, paternalistic source of the casuistical decisions that resolve the constant conflicts of function and jurisdiction throughout the system.[13]

This legitimacy derives from public consent, as appears in Suárez' recapitulation and elaboration of the Thomist principles. Power has a divine origin, and the sovereign people alienate it to their prince for the preservation of the society: "By contract, the prince is superior to the people" and "bound by his own law." When this law is unjust (that is, when it contradicts the "divine order"), when the majority has ceased to obey it, or when central authority is lacking, power reverts to the people, who originally were the depositories of this force originated by God. Thus, in the analysis of the normative basis of the patrimonial Spanish state, in particular as expressed by Suarez, reference is explicitly made to the limits set by religious tradition on the power of the king.

In its actual functioning, the Spanish imperial system appears to have been closer to the Thomistic model than to the Suarezian version. The power of the king's agents was not personal, but functional (as was that of the priest). We could apply to it the observations that Wolin makes on the power of the ecclesiastic: "It was exerted over a constituency that could only be the object and never the source of authority."[14] Although in the time of Charles V, the Spanish American settlers still had the right to elect their governor if the office became vacant (but only until the Crown had made a final nomination), this concession to popular sovereignty was gradually withdrawn. The directing principles of government were those of arbitrary patrimonial power, legitimized by the notion of the divine right of kings. These principles were retained and enforced without explicit mention of the "traditional safeguards" cited by Suarez.

Suarez' doctrine, however, was taught in colonial universities during the seventeenth and part of the eighteenth centuries. Morse suggests that its significance for the colonies lies beyond the apparent kinship with the theories of the Enlightenment. Its inconsistencies result in a particular view of "man, society and

---

[13] Morse, "The Heritage . . .," p. 156. Our discussion of the additions made by Suárez to the Thomist doctrine follows closely Morse's presentation in "The Heritage . . .," pp. 154-55.

[14] Op. cit., p. 137.

government" which is still relevant in the context of today's Latin America. In the words of Paul Janet:

> The Scholastic doctrines of the XVIth century [are] incoherent doctrines in which are united . . . democratic and absolutist ideas, without the author seeing very clearly where the former or the latter led him. . . . These principles [popular sovereignty, the exclusion of the doctrine of divine law, the insistence on unanimous consent as the foundation of society] serve only to allow him immediately to effect the absolute and uncondition alienation of popular sovereignty into the hands of one person. . . . As a guarantee against an unjust law, he offers only a disobedience both seditious and disloyal.[15]

Wolin also suggests a relation between the Christian medieval tradition and eighteenth century ideas: something of the Christian notion of the <u>corpus mysticum</u>, later recaptured in the notion of <u>corpus politicum</u>, reappears in Rousseau's conception of the community. Later still, "these ideas recur in the romantic and nationalistic literature of the XIXth century."[16] In the words of Mazzini: "A country must have a single government. The politicians, who call themselves federalists . . . would dismember the country, not understanding the idea of Unity."[17]

    Without discounting the direct inspiration that the leaders of Spanish American independence found in the Enlightenment and later in romantic thought, we would suggest the following: The idea of national unity, as the non-rational cementing force of a community governed by a strongly centralized state, is embryonically contained, as a secular derivation, in the Thomistic tradition, which was so influential in shaping the political conceptions of imperial Spain. Despite the withdrawal of Spain (and the rejection of all the aspects of its rule by the rebels), we can posit a kind of kinship between the centralizing efforts of the Independence leaders--often expressed in the articulate defense of dictatorial power--and the political philosophy of the regime to which they had been subjected for so long.[18] This point, how-

---

[15]<u>Histoire de la science politique dans ses rapports avec la morale</u> (3rd ed.; Paris, 1887), II, p. 76, quoted in Morse, "The Heritage . . .," p. 155.

[16]<u>Op. cit.</u>, p. 133.

[17]Giuseppe Mazzini, <u>The Duties of Man and Other Essays</u>, quoted in Wolin, <u>op. cit.</u>, p. 133.

[18]This is simply another element that could be added to the argument presented by Morse in the above quoted study.

ever, exceeds the scope of our present discussion.

The inconsistencies of Suarez' doctrine must be related to the context in which they were conceived and where they found such profound resonances. The reconciliation of principles that established the supremacy of "natural law" with the defense of patrimonial absolutism was more difficult in theory than it was divorced from the reality of sixteenth-century Spain. In effect, as we said before, "natural law" was the law of God, embodied in His church. Philip II, by his militancy on behalf of the True Faith, had achieved an identification between the interests of the Church and the interests of the monarchy. Says Romero:

> His reign was increasingly converted into a theocracy, and the Church acquired an influence that was scarcely contained by the king's prestige and stubbornness. . . . As the doctrinaire support of royal authority, the Church in the colony was the depository of the juridical and moral principles that the Crown upheld. The Church, in this capacity, . . . received dictatorship over spiritual affairs from the Spanish State.[19]

However, the opposite argument may be maintained. By espousing the interests of the Church, the Spanish king consolidated both the spiritual and temporal basis of his rule. As early as 1492, Pope Alexander VI awarded "all islands and mainlands west and south toward the Indies, provided they were not already possessed by another Christian prince," to the king, for him to spread the Christian faith. Later, as a compensation for this task, Popes Alexander and Julius II conferred control over the tithes levied in the Indies and the right of patronage in the New World on Ferdinand and his successors.

The Church in Spanish America became, by this token, an integral part of the power of the state. It enjoyed, it is true, the special privileges of a "state within a state," in compensation for the spiritual authority it provided as a buttress to the power of the king. However, the jurisdictional disputes between state and church are more adequately described as particular cases of the constant jurisdictional frictions that arise within a patrimonial bureaucratic system than as conflicts between separate powers. The king, not the Church, was the spiritual and political symbol of unity. The heterogeneous whole of the Spanish empire was held together by the common loyalty and allegiance owed to his person and to his power sanctioned by the Church. Thus, in sixteenth-century Spain, an explicit religious ideology re-elaborated the traditional tenets of royal absolutism, bringing an ideologic

---

[19] Op. cit., pp. 16 and 32.

THE STRUCTURAL AND NORMATIVE CHARACTERISTICS

justification to the predominant patrimonial conceptions. The latter, however, showed strong affinities with the more mundane theories that translate into "modern" economic terms the imperatives of arbitrary patrimonialism.

As we said before, for Weber the patrimonial state depends largely on the existence of large-scale commerce and on its control of this source of revenue. Thus, the economic theories that Adam Smith named "mercantilism" seem particularly well-fitted to the power structure of a "modern," i.e., bureaucratic-patrimonial, state. Economic conceptions represent an important element of the bureaucratic-patrimonial configuration. In the case which concerns us here, the mercantilist structure derived its <u>raison d'être</u> from the existence of a vast colonial empire which had to be kept under the economic and financial control of the Crown. Accordingly, a discussion of the economic aspects of patrimonialism will lead us to the central theme of this paper--a precise consideration of the application of the bureaucratic-patrimonial model to Spanish America.

ECONOMIC CONCEPTIONS: SPANISH MERCANTILISM

Mercantilism, as an economic theory, represents, in Weber's words, "a revolution in the financial policies of the European states," brought about by the "awakened capitalistic organization of industry, the bureaucratic rationalization of patrimonial power, and the ever-growing monetary demands of the external, military, and internal administrations." In this sense (and especially as it was conceived in sixteenth-century England), mercantilism is accompanied by the emergence of a powerful national state: transposing into the political sphere the acquisitiveness of early capitalism, its aim is "to strengthen abroad the power of state direction." The connection between this economic conception and the structure of patrimonial power appears quite clear. The power of the king is to be strengthened directly through the increase of his revenues and indirectly through the increase of the contributive capacities of the population (hence the stress on production). If, in early stages, mercantilism can appear to be geared solely toward the accumulation of bullion for the king's treasury, this cannot be the aim of the relatively modern patrimonial powers in an age of commercial expansion. Trade, as we have said before, aids in the growth of bureaucratic-patrimonial states, and commercial capitalism and state-oriented capitalism thrive under arbitrary patrimonialism. The latter, in Weber's words, "makes available the entire expanse of the sovereign's free will as an exploitable field for the formation of a patrimony," unlike the feudal structure of power which, "with its well circumscribed rights and duties, generally operates as a stabilizing influence, not only on the whole economic system, but also on the

SPANISH BUREAUCRATIC-PATRIMONIALISM IN AMERICA

division of individual patrimonies."[20]

Mercantilism, as an alliance of the state with the interests of commercial capitalism, tends toward two forms. The first is monopolistic mercantilism, where the purely fiscal orientation prevails and where new industries, based on the concession of a monopoly by the state, are submitted to strict state control. In this case, the system operates as a force which creates and stabilizes a new <u>Stand</u> order and is challenged, from outside the system of state monopolies, by emerging entrepreneurial groups. The second form is national mercantilism, which builds up a protectionist system for the national industries that already exist.

The Spanish system, although occasionally trying to eradicate some colonial industries which competed with the peninsular producers, came closer to the first form than the second. The core of the system was the monopoly on trade with the Indies, reserved, by royal will, to the powerful <u>Consulados</u> or merchant guilds. The state, moreover, had direct monopolies on mercury (essential in the production of silver, and thus a means of control on the distribution of this precious ore), gunpowder, salt, tobacco, etc., which, with the numerous taxes, provided a profitable source of revenue for the treasury. The mining industry was regulated, throughout the sixteenth century, by several codes of law. It was, however, backward and hazardous. In 1777, the <u>Real Cuerpo de Mineria</u> (mining guild) composed of a central tribunal in Mexico and provincial courts in each mining district, to which the mine-owners and operators elected their representatives, attempted to give it a comprehensive structure. The enlightened central supervision reflected a growing preoccupation with economic stagnation and a desire to bolster lagging production.

The mercantilist system, based on the principles of imperial control, proved to be the weakest aspect of the patrimonial

---

[20]Weber adds that this very arbitrariness is adverse to the growth of industrial capitalism, which for him, as we know, needs to rely on a formalized and calculable body of law. In the case of England, commercial capitalism based on monopolies granted by the state was challenged by the emergence of industrial entrepreneurship. This argument is documented by the recent study of an economist on the industrial revolution in England: Paul Bairoch, <u>Révolution industrielle et sous-développement</u> (Paris: IEDES, 1963). The controversial theoretical distinctions between feudalism, capitalism, and the questioned transitional stage of commercial capitalism are discussed in Maurice Dobb, <u>Studies in the Development of Capitalism</u> (rev. ed.; New York: International Publishers, 1963), and, in particular, in <u>The Transition from Feudalism to Capitalism</u>, by Paul Sweezy <u>et al</u>. (New York: Science and Society, 1963).

THE STRUCTURAL AND NORMATIVE CHARACTERISTICS

rule. To be successful, the system required both naval supremacy and an expanding market in Spain capable of absorbing the colonial output and, in turn, of satisfying the demands of colonial markets. In the eighteenth century, Spain had been completely displaced in both fields by England. The ever-growing contraband trade created new groups having semi-monopolies which prevented the colonists from obtaining the profits to be expected from free trade. At the same time, the monopolistic merchants of the Consulados had become --with the economic decay of Spain--mere intermediates between the colonies and the European markets and manufacturers. Their control resided in the abusive taxes they levied at both ends of the commercial circuit. The spreading venality and corruption of even the high colonial officials revealed that the system was doomed.

The reform of the intendentes in 1786 (see page 79) was meant to forestall this demise. It reflected both the more progressive mercantilistic conceptions of the Bourbons and an advance toward effective bureaucratic centralization corresponding to the heyday of the French state under Louis XIV. Brought to Spain (and hence to America) by the new dynasty, the new principles of organization were never fully enforced. The period of adjustment and conflict between the "old" and the "new" bureaucracies was still in course when the struggle for independence broke out.

In the long run, the Spanish imperial system failed. However, for more than three centuries, the American territories were subjected to a structure of government and administration which can be defined as patrimonial and bureaucratic. This structure, legitimized by a tradition expressed in the Thomist and neo-scholastic doctrines, was already apparent in Spain at the time of the Conquest. Later in the sixteenth century, when the Crown no longer had to reckon at home with the challenge posed by the nobility or the urban bourgeoisies, this model of government-- expressed in the economic sphere by the mercantilist theory--was even more forcefully brought to bear upon the New World.

Conquest was, from the beginning, an urban-centered enterprise, a factor which helped the Crown to curb the feudal "centrifugal" tendencies of the conquistadors and submit them to its administrative power. The remoteness of the new kingdoms, it is true, could have worked against the consolidation of patrimonial rule. And, indeed, we shall see how many of the contradictions and weaknesses of the bureaucratic system stemmed from this important fact. However, the Crown enjoyed the powerful alliance of the Church. While the power of the latter limited royal arbitrariness, the Crown found in the ecclesiastic hierarchy a group of auxiliaries free of dynastic intentions, not striving toward hereditary appropriation (a type of support often sought in the patrimonial monarchies studied by Weber). In addition, the remoteness of the provinces, by the divorce it effected between the original situation of the functionary at home (as a noble, a landed baron, a <u>grandee</u> of Spain, a military leader, etc.) and his power of office, countervailed the tendency toward decentralization of royal power. In spite of the difficulties of control it implied, the remoteness, in this case, contributed to the separation between private and public spheres characteristic of patrimonial bureaucracies dependent upon an arbitrary power. The separation of the functionary from his jurisdiction was furthered, as we shall see, by rules that guaranteed the prevalence of royal control.

However, the tendency toward the constitution of other patrimonies, independent from the power of the king and enjoying autonomy, was never completely overcome in those parts of the empire where royal power--in the person of the king's most reliable representatives--never reached or was weakest. The central power took various measures to countervail the flight of town-dwellers toward their country estates or toward the frontiers in its struggle against the "centrifugal local tendencies," but these were only partially successful.[21] In addition, the Crown clung, in principle, to its shaky control of the commercial system as a means of maintaining the subordination of the colonists who produced for an international market.

The following description of the imperial bureaucracy will illustrate some additional characteristics of Spanish rule in the American context, and will point out the lines of conflict that will help us to understand its final recession.

---

[21]See Morse, "Urbanization in Latin America," p. 38, and "Some Characteristics of Latin American Urban History," <u>American Historical Review</u>, LXVII, 2, January, 1962, pp. 317-38.

II

THE IMPERIAL BUREAUCRACY IN AMERICA: ORGANIZATION AND PRACTICE

STRUCTURAL SAFEGUARDS OF PATRIMONIAL RULE

The diagrams on the following pages show the complex organizational structure of Spanish colonial administration. Some aspects of the colonial administration require detailed discussion. Before discussing them, however, it will be useful to recall the main phases of the establishment of royal control over the new territories.

In the first phase, conquest was carried on as a purely private enterprise, with little financial or other participation by the Crown. The king's prerogatives, nonetheless, were at least nominally asserted; the impresario of the venture, usually a military leader, signed a contract with the king--the capitulacion --"in which were set down the rights reserved to the King in the new territories to be occupied, and the privileges conceded to the participants in recompense for their investment and the personal risks involved. . . . The founders and governors of the new colonies . . . often bore the title of adelantados, roughly equivalent to the Portuguese donatario."[1] This medieval Castilian distinction was revived to sanction the contribution of private enterprise in the establishment of the "new frontier" of Castile overseas. "The governorship of the territories subdued, with proprietary rights" was thus granted "for one or two lives, or sometimes in perpetuity."[2] However, the age of the adelantados was short because "in spite of these privileges so lavishly bestowed," says Haring, "colonization and administration in America were conceived from the very beginning as a function primarily of the State."[3] From 1530 onward, the absolutist crown of Castile undertook to limit or revoke the authority of the first governors, which threatened to encroach upon its own sovereignty. The audiencia of Mexico was established in 1528, and, in 1535, Antonio de Mendoza arrived as the first viceroy of New Spain. Soon after,

---

[1]C. H. Haring, The Spanish Empire in America (New York: Harcourt, Brace & World, Inc., 1963), pp. 19-22.

[2]Ibid., p. 20.

[3]Ibid., p. 169.

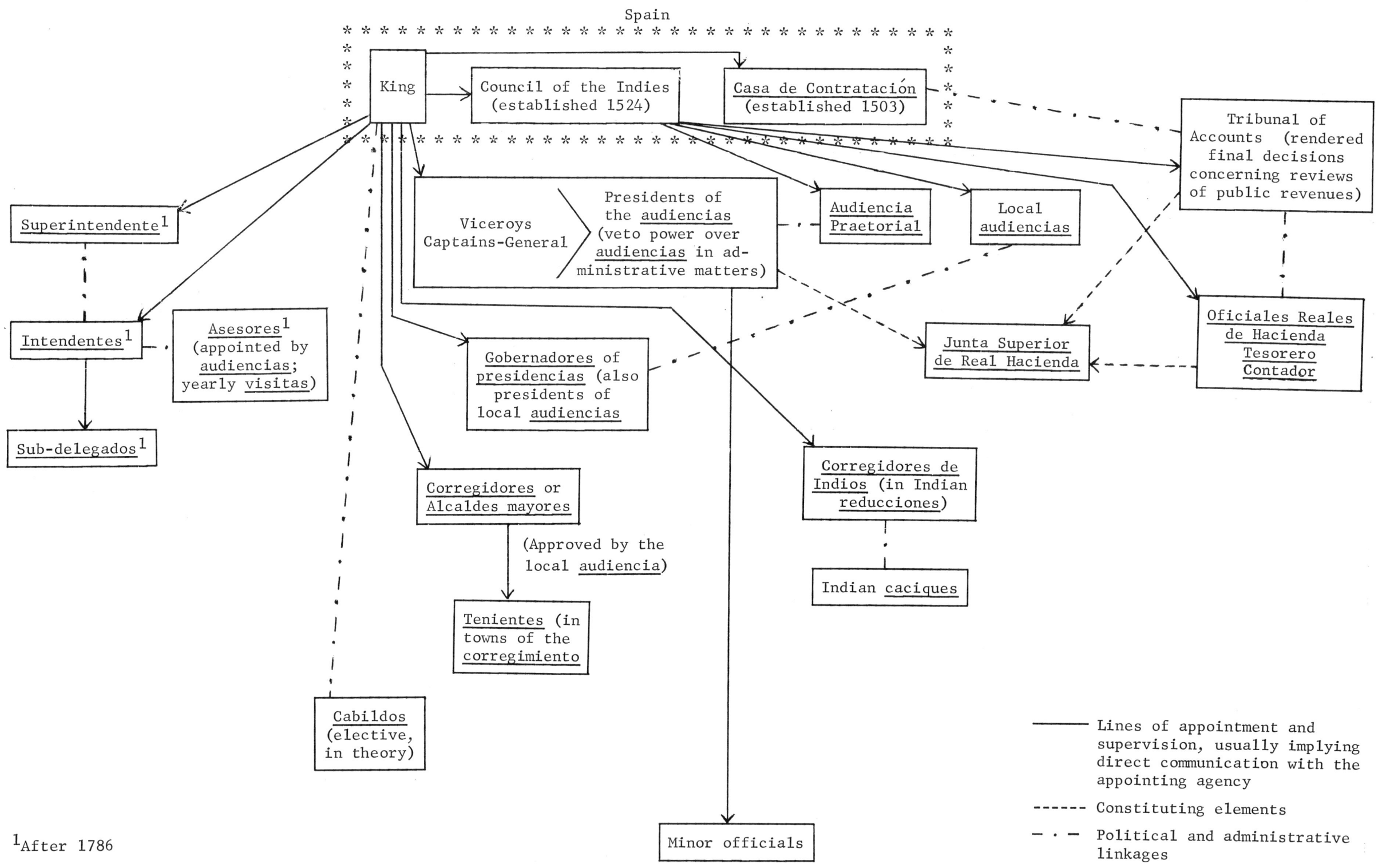

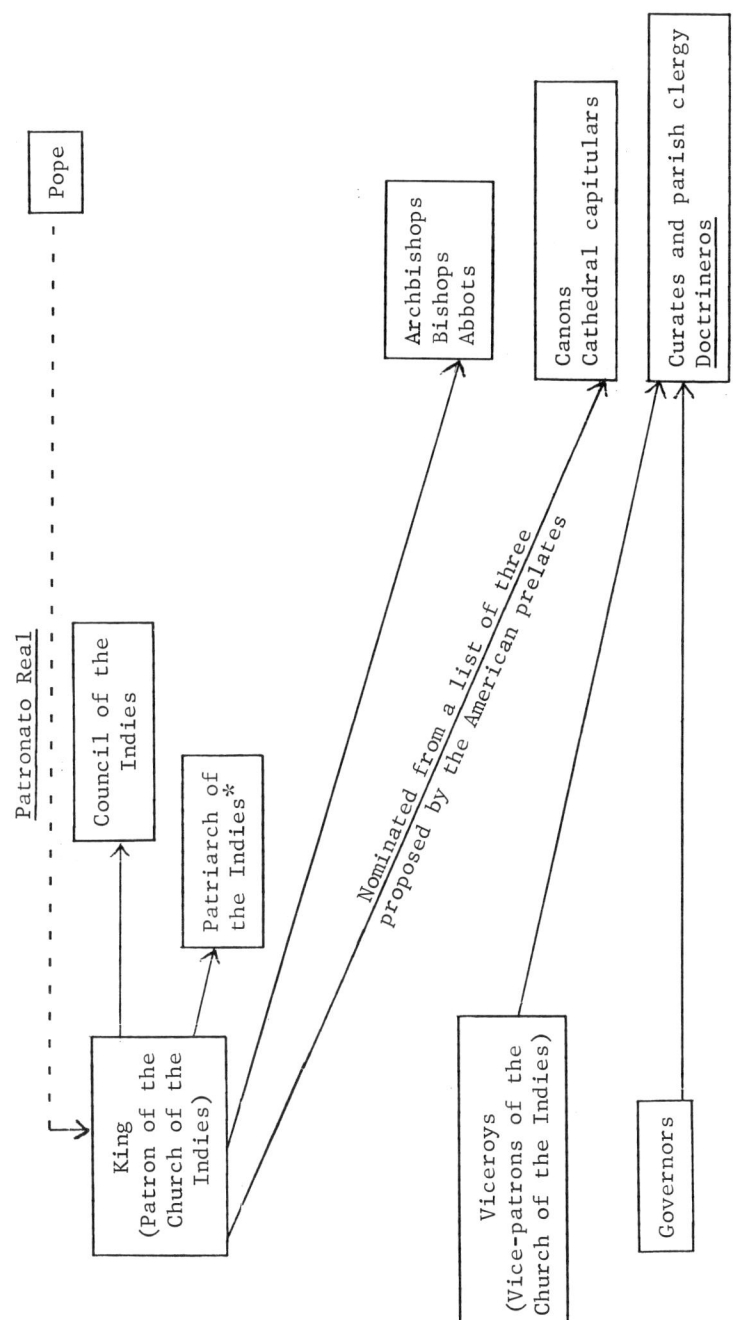

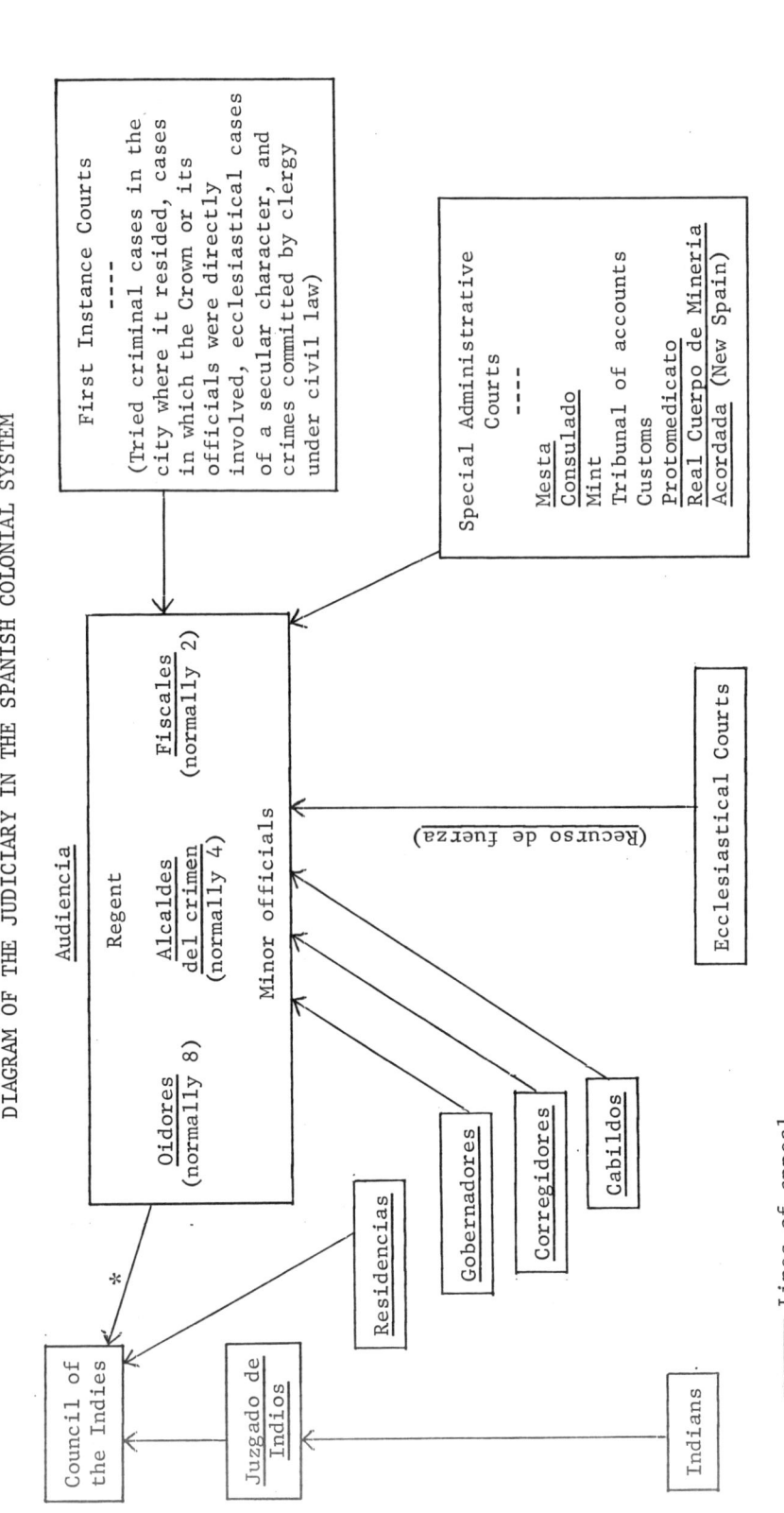

THE IMPERIAL BUREAUCRACY IN AMERICA

in 1544, Blasco Núñez Vela arrived in Peru "with a special mandate to enforce the New Laws intended to abolish Indian servitude. . . . With him came the first royal tribunal to be established in South America, the viceregal audiencia of Lima."[4]

Formally, the old territorial jurisdictions of the adelantados and the title of governor passed into the royal system of administration. However, once the phase of semi-autonomy was definitively closed, the architecture of colonial government was designed to consolidate the absolute power of the king, assisted by his Council of the Indies. Throughout the sixteenth century, a series of laws, most notably those of 1542, 1550, and 1573, laid out the framework of the system, each one representing a further attempt to curb the feudalistic power of the wealthier colonists. In 1681, the monumental Recopilación de Leyes de los reynos de las Indias summed up two centuries of legislation so meticulous that some of the laws "provide that there be a clock in the Casa de Contratacion of Seville . . .; that powder should not be wasted in salutes; or that the judges of Manila should not receive as gifts the chickens they consume or even purchase them at low prices."[5]

However, we are not concerned here with the particulars of the bureaucratic organization, but with its guiding principles. A "constant confusion between the fundamental laws and the details which in the modern age have been entrusted to the regulatory power"[6] reflects clearly the notions of government which prevailed in the early stages of royal absolutism, and the particular orientations of the Crown towards its colonial possessions and its agents overseas. The assertion of royal supremacy was expressed in the paternalistic, punctilious regulation of the smallest details of colonial life and administration: it wrapped up the royal agents in an enormous body of legislation that has been defined as "an unequal system, with assertions of high ideals surrounded by a network of mistrust."[7] In this way the Crown effectively curtailed the initiative of its officials.

Indeed, mistrust toward its own agents appears as one of the main traits of bureaucratic patrimonialism. It was reinforced from the start by unfortunate experiences with too powerful gov-

---

[4]Ibid., p. 83.

[5]Niceto Alcalá Zamora, Impresiones generales acerca de las Leyes de Indias (Buenos Aires, 1942), pp. 21-22. Quoted in Haring, op. cit.

[6]Ibid., p. 21.

[7]Ibid., p. 22.

SPANISH BUREAUCRATIC-PATRIMONIALISM IN AMERICA

ernors. As we pointed out before, America was too distant, too unknown, and too important for the Crown to permit, at least in theory, any degree of independence. The patterns of government and administration of Castile, and the trends toward arbitrary patrimonialism that we described earlier, were thus forcefully projected on the newfound lands. As Philip II made explicit in 1571:

> [B]ecause the kingdoms of Castile and the Indies belong to one crown and their laws and manner of government ought therefore to be as alike as possible, the members of our council shall try, in the laws and institutions which they may establish for those states, to reduce the form and manner of their government to the style and order by which are ruled and governed the realms of Castile and Leon so far as may be permitted by the diversity and difference of the lands and peoples.[8]

The relations between the king and his Council of the Indies (typical of "cabinet justice" as described by Weber) thus stood as a general model for the relations between the viceroy and the _audiencia_ in the colonies. The viceroy (or captain-general, where there was no viceroy) acted as the supreme coordinator of the complicated and overlapping hierarchies of colonial government. Although the viceroy "shared virtually all [his] powers with the audiencia as a council of state,"* the ultimate decision was almost always in his hands. The viceroy decided whether a case that came before the _audiencia_ was administrative or judicial and, as president of the high court, could bring all his personal influence to bear on the important cases. He, and he only, had power to appoint officers to posts which became vacant (until the nomination from Spain arrived). As vice-patron of the Church of the Indies, he appointed applicants to minor ecclesiastical offices. These appointments, as well as those in the lay hierarchy, were made from lists of three candidates provided by the chiefs of the various governing agencies (or by the American prelates). In matters of policy, "all ordinances issued by the viceroy, the _audiencia_ or lesser authorities, required royal confirmation. But while those of the viceroy or the _audiencia_ might be put into effect immediately, those of governors or municipalities required first the approval of the viceroy before enforcement and ultimately royal sanction."[9]

---

*My emphasis.

[8] Quoted in Haring, _op. cit._, pp. 5-6.

[9] _Ibid._, p. 111.

THE IMPERIAL BUREAUCRACY IN AMERICA

This brief description of the role of the viceroy suggests the contradictions inherent in viceregal power. While the viceroy's authority was undoubtedly supraordinate with regard to the other royal agencies in the colonies, "<u>the only real centralization was in the king and his council in Spain.</u>"*10 All the important officers were nominated or dismissed by the king. Therefore, the viceroy had little effective control over subordinates because they did not receive their tenure or authority from him.

Only routine activities were entirely in the hands of the viceroys or captains-general, but even here, as we have already indicated, a singular minuteness characterized the instructions issued by Spain, even in minor matters of administration. With respect to matters of main policy, the representatives of the Crown were mere executors of its political directives. Moreover, the system formally became more autocratic as time went on, with the progressive bureaucratization of the system continuing from the time of the first Hapsburgs to the administrative reforms of the Bourbons.

Within the general pattern of distrust by a Crown so jealous of its prerogatives, it is perhaps not surprising that

> the Hapsburgs did not, as a rule, take kindly to subordinates of the brilliant or inventive sort, who wanted to strike out on lines of their own. The official whom they preferred was the hard-working, competent, but obedient type, who would faithfully discharge the duties laid upon him, and send back for fresh instructions in any case of doubt. . . . The distance from Spain, the slowness of communications, the new conditions of which Europe was necessarily in densest ignorance, all rendered supervision from home exceedingly difficult, and offered the greatest temptation for independent action; it was therefore doubly essential that the crown be certain of the men that it placed there.[11]

This quotation suggests that certain discrepancies between principle and practice were imbedded in the system. However, we shall deal at greater length in a later paragraph with the ambiguities inherent in the Spanish colonial administration. For our present purposes, it is sufficient to note the emergence of a class of career bureaucrats in accordance with the rules of patri-

---

*My emphasis.

[10] Ibid., p. 112.

[11] Roger B. Merriman, <u>The Rise of the Spanish Empire in the Old World and in the New</u> (New York: Macmillan, 1936), Vol. III, p. 649.

monial selection described in the first chapter. John Leddy Phelan, who has analyzed the Spanish imperial framework in terms of the sociology of organizations, suggests that the Spaniards who monopolized all the important colonial offices "were motivated . . . by personal involvement in the system and its welfare."[12] Chosen (in theory) because they enjoyed the king's confidence, they were controlled by a series of incentives and penalties. Obviously, in this bureaucratic organization, the main incentive was promotion within the hierarchy, but also a favored geographical location was desired, which brought the organization close to the classic prebendal type.

As for control, the principal formal instruments were the *residencia* and the *visita*. The *residencia* goes back to 1501, when Nicolas de Ovando was instructed to conduct a judicial review of the conduct of his predecessor in Hispaniola, the Marques de Bobadilla. It was an extension to America of the practice systematically employed in Castile to control the office of *corregidor*, and was applied to all civil servants (with the exception of the clergy) at the end of their terms of office. "[T]he *residencia* of officials appointed by the Crown was entrusted to judges nominated in the Council of the Indies," while "in the case of officials appointed in America, the nominating agency named the judge of residence."[13] For those officials who had life tenure, the *residencia* was to be conducted (in principle) every five years. The penalties, writes Haring, were "heavy fines, confiscation of property, imprisonment, or all three." The *residencia* was a public trial, ultimately modified and then terminated by the Council of the Indies, to whom appeal was carried by the officers nominated in Spain. (The *audiencia* of the district was presumably a court of appeal from sentences pronounced by judges appointed in the Indies.)

The *visita*, on the contrary, was a secret investigation which could apply either to a single official or region or to an entire viceroyalty or captaincy-general. For local *visitas*, the commissioners were chosen by the viceroy or captain-general in consultation with the *audiencia*. While these local inspectors had purely investigatory duties and "were strictly forbidden to supplant in any way officials whose acts they were sent to examine," the *visitadores* sent from Spain obviously had greater and more far-reaching authority. Although the viceroy was subject to

---

[12]"Authority and Flexibility in Spanish Imperial Bureaucracy," Administrative Science Quarterly, Vol. 5, 1960.

[13]For a detailed description of these procedures, see Haring, op. cit., pp. 138-46. The following discussion is based primarily upon Haring's account.

THE IMPERIAL BUREAUCRACY IN AMERICA

the visita only in his capacity as president of the audiencia, he and the presidents of audiencias "were expected to aid [the visitador] in all ways possible." The visitor-general "had authority to call before him anyone he saw fit," to inspect the records of the audiencia, and to sit through its sessions. Even though the Council reviewed the reports and decided on the action to be taken, the visitador had some independent powers:

> Ministers of justice or officers of the exchequer found to have committed grave offenses against the public weal, might immediately be suspended from office, as well as officials who impeded the visitador in the performance of his duties. If it seemed desirable, they might be exiled from the province or sent to Spain.

As far as his mission went, the visitador was authorized to proceed with complete independence, even though appeal from his decisions could always be carried to the Council in Spain.

Another practice aimed at preventing abuse and malversations was an inventory of personal wealth required of many officials prior to their taking office. This measure applied both to the corregidores (the local agents who were the most difficult to control, as proved by their infamous reputation) and to the treasury officials. It was complemented by a bond these officials were required to furnish and deposit in the chief town of their jurisdiction. Furthermore, all the Crown's agents were subject to a set of restrictions intended to secure their impartiality and to prevent malpractice in their service. The general policy of appointing Spaniards to the principal positions was designed to keep royal agents free of community attachments and preferences.

> Viceroys, judges and their children were not allowed to marry in the colonies without regal consent. They might not engage in business of any sort, borrow or lend money, and neither they nor their wives or children might own real estate in the cities in which they resided or anywhere else within their jurisdiction. They might not even legally exchange hospitalities, act as godfather in families outside their own official circle, or be present at marriages or funerals. If permitted to marry within the community while they held office, they were generally transferred to another province.[14]

The same applied to other, less important representatives. When Creoles were appointed, they were invariably transferred to another district than that where they lived. Furthermore, "viceroys or

---

[14] Ibid., p. 126.

SPANISH BUREAUCRATIC-PATRIMONIALISM IN AMERICA

presidents, in appointing to corregimientos, were forbidden to name relatives within the fourth degree of any of the more important officials of the province."[15] The corregidor himself could not name any of his subordinates from among his relatives to the fourth degree. These regulations--typical of the patrimonial structure of power--may seem impossible to enforce; they contributed, however, in the American context, to the accentuation of the caste characteristics of a class of foreign-born bureaucrats who were to remain as remote as possible from the actual life of the community.

Finally, the structure of the system of government and administration provided another type of check on possible abuses of power. A principle of rule which reflected the general distrust of the royal power toward its representatives was applied through a division of responsibility, aimed at balancing forces between the various hierarchies. As Professor Haring has so clearly described its practice,

> Spanish imperial government was one of checks and balances; not secured as in many modern constitutional states by a division of powers, legislative, judicial, executive, but by a division of authority among different individuals or tribunals exercising the same powers. There was never a clear-cut line of demarcation between the functions of various governmental agencies dealing with colonial problems [as we have briefly indicated with regard to viceroys and audiencias]. On the contrary, a great deal of overlapping was deliberately fostered to prevent officials from unduly building up personal prestige or engaging in corrupt or fraudulent practices.[16]

The above description is not intended to give a comprehensive view of the Spanish colonial bureaucracy. Several elements neglected here will, however, be considered in a later discussion of colonial society. Thus, the intendentes, who replaced governors and corregidores after Charles III's administrative reforms at the end of the eighteenth century, will appear in their relationship with local powers and, in particular, with the cabildos. The latter constituted, it is true, the smallest and lowest administrative units of the Spanish system, but they also "were the only institutions in which the Creole or Spanish-American element in society was largely represented."[17] As such they pertain

---

[15]Ibid., p. 129.

[16]Ibid., pp. 112-13.

[17]Ibid., p. 147.

THE IMPERIAL BUREAUCRACY IN AMERICA

closely, in our opinion, to another topic--namely, the relationships between society and the colonial system of government. As suggested above, we have tried here merely to outline the main characteristics of the Spanish patrimonial bureaucracy in America.

Composed as it was of "multiple, partly independent and partly inter-dependent hierarchies,"[18] with each echelon able to communicate directly with the vertex or to appeal many of the decisions of superior magistrates, the Spanish colonial system became a stereotyped, procrastinating bureaucracy. There were, of course, various individual exceptions. Nevertheless, it is true to say that the energy of the superior officials was more often than not wasted in endless jurisdictional disputes or questions of precedence. The reform of the intendentes--an attempt to provide "for greater centralization of functions in the provinces and greater uniformity, if not simplicity, of administration"[19]-- indicates, as we suggested before, the inefficiency that paralyzed the bureaucracy toward the end of the eighteenth century. Considered in terms of its general goals, the system was ambiguous and often dysfunctional (as we shall try to point out in the following pages), even though, at another level of analysis, it was a perfect expression of the patrimonial principles upon which it was based. Power was, in effect, centralized in the extreme at the vertex of the system, but, for practical purposes, ineffectively delegated. In the words of Professor Morse: "The multiplicity of judicial systems underscored the static, functionally compartmented nature of society. The fact that they--like the several hierarchies of lay and clerical administrators--constantly disputed each other's sphere of influence only served to reaffirm the King's authority as ultimate reconciler."[20]

With a hierarchy subordinate to its "prime mover," the king, the system also had, in principle, an ideological unity, a non-rational cement--namely, the Catholic faith. The juridical doctrine of the Patronato Real sanctioned the alliance of church and royalty. On the one hand, the king could rely upon the formidable buttress of a national church incorporated into or adjacent to the lay system of administration. On the other hand, as the secular head of the Church of the Indies, he was committed to the supramundane ends of evangelization and the spread of the Christian

---

[18]Phelan, op. cit., p. 53.

[19]Haring, op. cit., p. 136.

[20]"Toward a Theory of Spanish American Government," reprinted from The Journal of the History of Ideas, XV, 1954, under the title "Political Theory and the Caudillo" in Hugh H. Hamill, ed., Dictatorship in Spanish America (New York: A. Knopf, 1965).

SPANISH BUREAUCRATIC-PATRIMONIALISM IN AMERICA

religion. The relationship was, in this respect, dualistic: "The Church defended the divine sanctity of kings; the Crown upheld the ecumenical authority of the Roman Catholic Church."[21] The primary motive force underlying the conquest may not have been religious. However, by reinforcing the transcendental basis of royal authority, the Church contributed to the enormous task of modeling the new territories upon the Spanish cultural patterns.[22] In the words of Fernando de los Rios:

> Spain was impelled to two kinds of militant action at that momentous period of her history: the one militarist, the other spiritual, both combative and eager to conquer. . . . A realization of that permanent interrelation between two organisms, each of which depended for its existence on absorbing a part of the vital juice of the other, is quite fundamental for the understanding of Spanish colonization.[23]

Although these brief considerations enable us to complete the characterization of the patrimonial order and its Thomistic ideology, the coexistence of different orientations at the vertex of the system had direct political consequences. Royal patron of the Church of the Indies by papal concession, the King of Spain

---

[21] Haring, op. cit., p. 166.

[22] However, formalistic, religious considerations were present from the beginning of the conquest, as proved by the important controversy on the "human status" of the Indians. The moral justification of the conquest and subjugation of the Indians was indeed a very serious issue in the period following the discovery. The requerimiento is a particularly striking illustration of the intertwining between the brutal motives for conquest and the need to comply with universalistic religious criteria. This proclamation, demanding allegiance to the pope and the King of Castile, was read to the Indian tribes (often directly in Spanish!). "Every conquistador," says Haring, "was required to have it read to the Indians by a notary and through an interpreter, before their territory could legally be taken or hostilities against them be started." For more details, see Silvio Zavala, New Viewpoints on the Spanish Colonization of America (Philadelphia, 1943), Chaps. 1-4, and Lewis Hanke, "The Requerimiento and Its Interpreters," Revista de Historia de America, No. 1, p. 28.
   The religious tone of the conquest is further evidenced by the fact that the absolute supremacy of the Council of the Indies was called into question, in America, only with respect to the Inquisition, established by Philip II in 1569.

[23] "The Action of Spain in America," in Concerning Latin American Culture (New York: Columbia, 1940), p. 53.

THE IMPERIAL BUREAUCRACY IN AMERICA

was also the head of an empire, an economic and political enterprise organized on mercantilistic conceptions. The general edicts issued by the king and the Council of the Indies were often, as we shall see, mutually contradictory. This point allows us to return to the ambiguities of the bureaucratic system and to its actual functioning. And this, in turn, will introduce our discussion of the relations between government and society in Spanish America.

PRACTICAL ENCROACHMENTS UPON ARBITRARY PATRIMONIALISM

Up to now we have pointed out that the large areas of uncertainty allowed by the Spanish patrimonial system (because of its unclearly defined powers) curtailed the authority of its local agents. We have also said that, at least in theory, each governmental agency, including the cabildos, had the privilege to be in direct communication with the higher central authorities in Spain. Similarly, some wealthy and educated colonists maintained not infrequent correspondence with the Council of the Indies, as the archives of the Council bear witness. Even the Indian caciques were entitled (however illusory this privilege may have proved to be) to carry their complaints to the local audiencia over the head of their corregidor. In principle, then, the authoritative actions of the supraordinate officials could always be denounced by their subordinates to the supreme agencies in the metropolis. While this patrimonial principle opened a channel for voicing "the spirit of rivalry which animated the various parts of the colonial service," it also encouraged, theoretically, the expression of grievances: "The vociferous debates and generous legislation on the problems of labor and race relations in the sixteenth century are possibly the best examples of a readiness to hear complaints and react to pressure which is not usually associated with Spanish government."[24] In this highly centralized system, however, flexibility sprang more directly from other sets of conditions.

In the first place, the distance from Spain and the very slow pace of communications (in the sixteenth century, communications could take from six to eight months to reach Lima, for instance) necessarily favored the assumption of initiative by the viceroys and superior magistrates. Faced with an order from Spain that proved to be unfeasible or dangerous in the face of local conditions, the superior officials could revert to the traditional formula of Spanish administration: "I obey but do not execute."[25] By this means, they acknowledged the legitimate

---

[24]John Lynch, "The Crisis of Colonial Administration," reprinted in R. A. Humphreys and John Lynch, eds., The Origins of the Latin American Revolutions (New York: A. Knopf, 1965), pp. 113-14.

[25]The following discussion closely follows John Leddy Phelan's article cited in fn. 12 of this chapter.

power of the sovereign but postponed execution until their report on the actual local situation reached the Court. Given the very slow pace of feedback, this ensured the colonial agents a certain freedom to select their responses to orders. Presumably the new instructions from Spain reflected, to some extent at least, the opinion of the colonial officials. The procedure was used then, in effect, as "an institutional device for decentralizing decision-making."

In practice, then, the viceroy was enabled to judge the wisdom of directives. These directives often reflected the overall goal of the Spanish system of administration--ambiguity. "No clear-cut priority among the various standards was available for the agents," writes Phelan, with the notable exception of the Church: "The spiritual welfare of the natives and colonists was a clear-cut goal from which the Church could scarcely deviate, although various branches of the clergy clashed upon the means of reaching that goal." The king, in his capacity as apostolic vicar, had to respond to the pressure of Rome instigated by the missionaries who returned from America. It is debatable that the legislation protecting the Indians from the ruthless exploitation of the encomenderos was inspired by a purely humanitarian concern for the new souls gained to the true religion, but the New Laws of 1542 bear witness to this concern. On the other hand, the laws also reflect a more materialistic concern--namely, to curtail the excessive autonomy of the encomenderos. The violent reaction of the latter indicated their awareness of the king's underlying purposes and also showed what serious consequences the colonial officials had to face directly.[26]

The spiritual duty of the Royal Patron was perfectly blended with the desire to enforce his sovereignty and to preserve the Indian population as the "demographic and economic foundation of royal power in America." Demographic because, in the words of one of the preachers of Charles V, "la encomienda le quita al Rey lo que le hace gran señor, que es la muchedumbre del pueblo,"[27] and the extermination of the Indian race by the hardships to which it was subjected clearly threatened the power of the king, based as it was, in this pre-capitalist era, on area and numbers. Economic because the Indians paid a tribute to the Crown and, indirectly, were the necessary condition to a well-faring colonial

---

[26] See special appendix to this monograph on the Indians and Indian policy.

[27] "The encomienda deprives the king of that which makes him great, that is the number of the people." Quoted in Sergio Bagú, Estructura Social de la Colonia (Buenos Aires: Ateneo, 1952), p. 167. [My translation.]

THE IMPERIAL BUREAUCRACY IN AMERICA

economy, as was clearly indicated by New Spain's "century of depression," which, according to historians, originated with the death by epidemics of a great part of the Indian labor force.[28]

As the labor market tightened, the viceroy received the royal *cedulas* of 1601 and 1609, aimed at alleviating the Indians' burden. Faced with a seething revolt of the colonists in Mexico City, the local authorities gave priority to the general economic crisis rather than to the specific plight of the Indians. In other words, they chose, naturally enough, to stress the mercantile rather than the supposedly "spiritual" orientation of the system. This case illustrates what Phelan has called the "flexibility" of response of the colonial officials when confronted with conflicting or unclear standards. They were exposed to manifold pressures: the instructions from Spain and the contradictory orientations of the system to which they were committed; the need to abide by local conditions, public opinion, the influence of their peers and subordinates; their own assessment of possible sanctions if their decisions ultimately proved wrong or unwise. Flexibility, then, arose from the variety of possible responses. Moreover, by the selective evaluation of the contradictory directives they received,[29] the superior officials, adjusting to factual realities, necessarily generated "independent" authority within the tight formal framework of the system. As pointed out by Haring,

> there . . . grew up a substantial amount of customary law . . . derived from the jurisprudential practices of the times, which had a recognized legal force if accepted by the Crown and if no written legislation was applicable. Much of this customary jurisprudence developed from the modifications of royal orders by viceroys and captains-general to meet the exigencies of a local situation.[30]

The reverse of the medal was the possibility of disregarding royal mandates as well as general rules and regulations for everyday administration: the higher colonial officials, we are told, "often united with other officials in the neighborhood in a common con-

---

[28] In particular, see W. Borah, *New Spain's Century of Depression* (Berkeley and Los Angeles: University of California Press, 1951).

[29] Contradictory, as we have seen, since they reflected the difference of conception of the colonists and the Church with respect to the Indian question, the conflict between the king and his powerful American subjects, and, last but not least, the contradictions between the different objectives of the Crown itself.

[30] *Op. cit.*, p. 101.

SPANISH BUREAUCRATIC-PATRIMONIALISM IN AMERICA

spiracy to disregard restrictive laws . . ."[31] As Juan de Solorzano Pereira, one of the judges of the Lima *audiencia*, wrote in the sixteenth century: "The mandates of the princes themselves may be foolish, or some without warrant, and open a wide field to those who inhabit or govern [the provinces], to judge and hold lawful everything to which their whim urges or persuades them. For human temerity easily disregards that which is very distant."[32]

The principle of absolute royal authority and control was even further threatened by the pressing financial needs of the treasury and the rather short-sighted policies that resulted. Thus, before the end of the sixteenth century, the practice of selling public offices was extended to most municipal offices and to many posts connected with the mints, the exchequer, the minor non-judicial offices of the courts of law, etc. Under the reign of Charles II, even the offices in the Council of the Indies were sometimes sold. Of all these, however, the sale of municipal offices is particularly relevant to our discussion. In the colonies, the practice applied to minor positions and did not grant hereditary rights. The Crown, if it deemed it necessary, could always buy out the right of office (as it did, under Charles III, for instance, for the office of postmaster general in New Spain). Given the limited attributions of power to the *cabildos*, the selling of offices did not essentially encroach upon royal power; however, the sale of offices did provide a basis for the entrenchment of local privileges. By this means, the urban oligarchies could gain political control of the local, minor, administrative apparatus. According to an Argentine historian, a tradition of corrupt and non-accountable local governments originated in this practice: "The government, by selling offices, implicitly admitted that its affairs were exploitable, that they were articles of commerce."[33] And it is indeed an easy view to accept that offices thus bought--in addition to the social prestige they bestowed upon their occupants--were conceived also as investments to be amortized as rapidly as possible.

We can sum up by saying that, although observance of the royal will expressed in the law was written into every feature of the Spanish system of administration, together with an extremely punctilious type of legalism, the discrepancy between general orders and local conditions made deviations from principle very common. Moreover, the meticulousness of the regulations made

---

[31] *Ibid.*, p. 114.

[32] *Loc. cit.*

[33] J. A. Garcia, *La Ciudad Indiana* (3a ed.; Buenos Aires: Angel Estrada y Cia., n.d.), pp. 169-70. [My translation.]

THE IMPERIAL BUREAUCRACY IN AMERICA

them impossible to enforce. In the case of taxes, for instance, the younger Revillagigedo, viceroy of New Spain, remarked:

> It is . . . impossible for the taxpayer to have knowledge of every one of the contributions, to know clearly what he ought to pay, and how and why he ought to do so . . . [and he therefore all the more resents] the arbitrary methods of officials under a multitude of complicated rules, added to the unjust or improper manner in which subordinates are wont to conduct themselves. All this is extremely difficult to remedy when there are so many exactions, some of them so complicated and so difficult to determine that their collection has to be left to the discrimination of the collectors.[34]

Furthermore, if isolation from Spain was great, so was isolation between the different parts of the empire. To bring a complaint against a corregidor to the nearest audiencia, a plaintiff often had to face the hardships and the expenses of a trip that might take several months. The supraordinate authorities, then, could hardly control the local authorities. While it is true that changes in territorial organization were made in the second half of the seventeenth century (the multiplication of audiencias, captaincies-general, viceroyalties was part of the general effort to increase the possibilities of control), even so the Spanish system could not be made effective. It could not check the centrifugal tendencies of such an immense empire. However powerful its agents may have been, they could not muster enough forces to make their authority effective in all the areas of their jurisdiction.[35] Where the patrimonial rule could not reach, or where it failed, there was, then, a large degree of autonomy of the peripheral units. Isolation made them self-contained, with authority fragmented in the hands of the de facto rulers--that is, the provincial officials and the local "lords of the land."

---

[34]Instrucción, par. 1367-69. Quoted in Haring, op. cit., p. 285, note 12.

[35]Until the creation of professional armies (the first was created in New Spain in 1762) and of regular colonial militiae, the armed forces consisted only of the guard of the viceroy, "reinforced later by a company or two of infantry called compañías de palicio" (Haring, op. cit., p. 115). There also were urban militiae maintained by the merchant or craft guilds and local companies at the seaports and at the frontiers. "In time of danger . . . local forces were usually raised and armed for the emergency" (ibid.).

III

SPANISH BUREAUCRATIC-PATRIMONIALISM AND COLONIAL SOCIETY

We have tried to deal generally with the direct and indirect ways by which the patrimonial order--wedded, as we have seen, to a "Thomistic" political outlook--was actually imposed upon the new colonial societies. In defining the social groups that constituted these societies, we must bear in mind, in the first place, their relationship to the Spanish system of government. Some of the elements already presented will reappear in this discussion from another viewpoint. If our previous considerations were centered on the structure of the bureaucracy and the relations of its different agents with the "directing head," we will briefly consider here the class of career bureaucrats in relation to the other constitutive parts of the colonial society.

THE GROUPS DIRECTLY RELATED TO THE PATRIMONIAL STRUCTURE OF POWER

A. The Functionaries of the Crown: The gradual emergence of a class of career bureaucrats is inseparable from the process by which the Crown imposed control upon the conquerors and governors ad vitam of the first phase of colonial rule. A necessary feature of royal control, if it was to be effective, was, as we have seen, insulation of the royal functionaries from the rest of society. We have already referred to legislation that prevented career bureaucrats from engaging directly in business activities and establishing close links with local groups. Such rules were designed to secure the impartiality of their performance in office but, above all, to guarantee the priority of their commitment to the Crown and the imperial system of government. However difficult it may have been to enforce these rules, the bureaucratic pattern eliminated, for instance, the nepotistic practices that were so widespread in the first phase of the conquest. The civil servants "changed posts and could therefore take root in one place only with difficulty."[1]

---

[1]François Chevalier, "The Roots of Personalismo," reprinted in Hugh H. Hamill, ed., Dictatorship in Spanish America (New York: A. Knopf, 1965). Chevalier tells us that "in a case in Mexico in 1602, Guadalajara had only 160 households, but the President of the Audiencia there was surrounded by 46 relatives, and by a quantity of dependents who monopolized the offices and the most lucrative jobs of . . . New Galicia" (pp. 37-38).

SPANISH BUREAUCRATIC-PATRIMONIALISM AND COLONIAL SOCIETY

Obviously enough, deviations from the rules were very frequent, and the fringe benefits that could be obtained from the service were almost institutionalized in the system of promotion. The system itself, through its ambiguities, allowed, as we have seen, a substantial area of initiative and a redefinition of the amount of power it formally delegated. However, one point remained: the representatives of the Crown were not, as such, supposed to engage directly in what we shall call the "creative" tasks of the conquest. Discovery, expansion of the frontier, exploitation of the local resources were not directly part of their incumbency. They administered the patrimony of the supreme proprietor, the king, by granting concessions of land, allocating labor forces, and regulating exploited or prospected mines. Executors of the royal policy, they simply saw to establishing the king's rights to a portion of the wealth accumulated in the new territories.

In addition, in these highly hierarchized societies where all the parts were related to the integrating symbol of the Crown, the royal representatives were the center from which social prestige emanated. "The King," writes Morse, "was symbolic throughout his realm as the guarantor of status."[2] Thus, in the colonies, the viceroy, the captain-general, and the *audiencia* were the most visible marks of the social ordering, the witnesses to its reality. The brilliant social life of the old viceregal capitals revolved, naturally enough, around "the court," from which patterns of consumption and styles of life were learned and status derived. As Haring writes of the *audiencias*: "They helped to give to the cities in which they resided a cultural, military and economic preeminence which made them the nuclei of larger areas bounded together by a community of sentiments and interests."[3] Much more is suggested by this quotation than can be discussed until we return specifically to a consideration of urban life in the colonies. Here one point should be expressed, however. The royal representatives had an undoubted preeminence in colonial life. This preeminence, political and social, derived directly from the patrimonial structure. The "management of economic progress"-- in the pre-capitalistic sense of accumulation of land, serfs, bullion, and market-valuable products--was not as a rule in their hands (except for its military aspects) until the reform of the *intendentes*.

---

[2] R. Morse, "Toward a Theory of Spanish American Government," reprinted from *The Journal of the History of Ideas*, XV, 1954, under the title "Political Theory and the Caudillo" in Hugh H. Hamill, ed., *op. cit.*, p. 56.

[3] C. H. Haring, *The Spanish Empire in America* (Harcourt, Brace & World, Inc., 1963), p. 126.

SPANISH BUREAUCRATIC-PATRIMONIALISM IN AMERICA

B. The Clergy and Related Groups: A second group directly related to the "patrimonial order" was the clergy. Its situation was somewhat different from the bureaucracy, since the Church, incorporated as it was in an imperial structure, enjoyed the special prerogatives and privileges of "a state within a state." The members of the clergy were, in the first phases of the conquest, its spiritual arm, so to speak--the representatives and functional agents of the spiritual order in which the sanctity of the king's rights and the ultimate ideological justification of the conquest were rooted. The Crown imposed the presence of friars or priests at the side of the military leaders and explorers. Later, it followed the policy of "having a bishopric erected immediately upon the colonization of any new region."[4]

For the colonial societies, the powerful and wealthy Church, open to Creoles and even occasionally to some noteworthy Indians, "appeared as a secure refuge for those who did not find a place within the colonial economic pattern. . . . [T]he Church offered a secure and not too painstaking occupation to thousands of individuals in the active ages."[5] Thus, the remark that Calmon applied to Brazil holds true for Spanish America as well: "The elder of the sons of the senhor de engenho [plantation owner] inherited the occupation of his father; the second went to Coimbra to study; the third was destined for the ecclesiastic career."[6]

The development of the American clergy soon became so impressive that the Crown and even the pope tried to check the rapid increase.[7] In 1611, the Franciscans alone had 166 religious houses in New Spain; in 1614, of the 25,454 inhabitants of Lima, 2,518 (or ten percent of the population) were priests, canons, friars, or nuns. As a matter of fact, the main possibilities of careers open to the Creoles (although the modern concept of career is not quite applicable in this context) were either in the lower echelons of the colonial service or connected with the Church, directly or indirectly. The universities created in the sixteenth

---

[4]Ibid., p. 170.

[5]Sergio Bagú, Economía de la Sociedad Colonial (Buenos Aires: Ateneo, 1949), p. 91. [My translation.]

[6]Quoted by Sergio Bagú, Estructura Social de la Colonia (Buenos Aires: Ateneo, 1952), p. 94. [My translation.]

[7]Recopilación, lib. IV, tit. 12, ley 10. Cited in Haring, op. cit., p. 175. As early as 1535 the Crown decreed that lands in New Spain might be bestowed on conquistadors and other worthy settlers only on condition that they were never alienated to an ecclesiastic, a church, or a monastery.

SPANISH BUREAUCRATIC-PATRIMONIALISM AND COLONIAL SOCIETY

century were in the hands of the Dominicans or, above all, the Jesuits. These schools were established and sanctioned both by royal and pontifical decrees. Although they enjoyed, as relatively closed corporations, a certain degree of autonomy (which could also have been a reflection of the particular status of the Church), they were an integral part of the colonial system. Apart from the requisite of <u>limpieza de sangre</u> (purity of blood), the students had to prove that they were free from the taint of heresy. The professors, whose main reward was in terms of social prestige, since their salaries were extremely low, "had to take an oath to defend the doctrine of the Immaculate Conception, observe a modest conduct, and keep away from theatres, dances and other unseemly diversions."[8]

The ecclesiastic hierarchy was, then, recruited on a wider basis than the colonial service, and grounded on a very large class of American friars, clergymen, and prelates.[9] Through its virtual monopoly of education, and of most social services, the Church controlled many important positions within the social order. Furthermore (differing in this from the career bureaucracy), the Church, as a distinct institution, participated directly in the economic exploitation of the new continent. By its direct connection with the Indians through its mission of evangelization, the Church fulfilled another, more mundane, function. Its establishments at the outposts of the empire (the Jesuit and Franciscan missions in particular) were not only religious enterprises, but also "one of the most conspicuous pioneering devices of the Spanish government, a military and political agency designed to push back the frontiers, pacify the natives, and open the country to European occupation."[10]

Moreover, "the clergy shared in the use of forced labor in the form of the <u>mita</u> or the <u>repartimiento</u> as did the other Spaniards."[11] On the basis of Indian labor, the tithes it received

---

[8]Haring, <u>op. cit.</u>, p. 215.

[9]From the sixteenth century to 1813, only four of all the viceroys were American-born. They were the sons of Spanish officials in the colonies. Of the 602 captains-general, governors, and presidents, 14 were Creoles, as compared to the 105 Creoles among the 706 bishops and archbishops.

[10]See Herbert E. Bolton, "The Mission as a Frontier Institution in the Spanish-American Colonies," <u>American Historical Review</u>, XXIII, pp. 42-61.

[11]Haring, <u>op. cit</u>., p. 176. See also the special appendix on the Indians at the end of this paper.

from the Crown, and innumerable donations and bequests, the Church became the most wealthy corporation in the colonies. Some of its enterprises, primarily the remarkable achievements of the Jesuits in agricultural production and manufacturing based on the Indian crafts, can be considered as models of early capitalistic organization in Spanish America.[12] "The missions," writes Bagú, "provided manufactured articles in great quantities. . . . [T]hus, in the town of Potosi, one of the most rich and populous of the sixteenth century, the population consumed the greater part of the products of the neighboring Jesuitic missions."[13] Furthermore, in these economic systems where the opportunities for investment were scarce, there was little need for banking until the period of economic development in the second half of the eighteenth century. The Church, because of its enormous revenues, and because it functioned as a corporation, controlled most of the liquid capital. Thus, writes Haring, "when the improvident landowner needed to borrow, he applied to the monasteries. For they alone . . . had an accumulated surplus to invest. They were in a sense the banks of Spanish colonial America."[14]

The best proof of the enormous economic power of the Church is to be found in the exceptional measures that the Bourbons, in particular, took against the excessive numbers and wealth of the clergy.

> A decree of March 1717 declared that the number of friars was a burden upon the land, hindered the cultivation of the fields and the increase of public wealth, and that thereafter no conventual establishments were to be created in the Indies. In 1734 the Crown ordered, with the approval of Rome, that for ten years no one in New Spain be admitted under any pretext to a religious Order. Twenty years later, in 1754, the king expressly forbade any member of a religious Order to interfere in the drawing up of wills. . . . [I]n 1775 a decree was again issued forbidding confessors or their convents to be heirs or legatees.[15]

---

[12]For more details, see François Chevalier, Land and Society in Colonial Mexico (Berkeley: University of California Press, 1963). Excerpts from pp. 229-31 and 239-50 are reprinted under the title "The Formation of the Jesuit Wealth," in Magnus Mörner, ed., The Expulsion of the Jesuits from Latin America (New York: A. Knopf, 1965).

[13]Economía . . ., p. 90.

[14]Op. cit., p. 178.

[15]Ibid., pp. 176-77.

SPANISH BUREAUCRATIC-PATRIMONIALISM AND COLONIAL SOCIETY

The expulsion of the Jesuits in 1767 can also be partially interpreted as a consequence of their economic power and the influence they hence derived. In spite of the relative autonomy and the special status of the Church within the patrimonial Spanish order, the Crown, even in earlier years, was not in principle willing to tolerate an increase in the formidable power of its ally. It has to be borne in mind that the Church acted as a corporation, on its own behalf. The wealth it accumulated did not revert to society, nor was it taxable by the Crown, however vital its functions may have been for the empire. Economically, as the decree of 1717 stated, the Church was a burden to the commonwealth for two main reasons--"the acquisition of so much of the best agricultural land by way of benefactions, purchase or mortgage, and the system of ecclesiastical taxation, especially the tithe . . . [which] amounted to a ten percent income tax collected at the source of agricultural and pastoral industries."[16] In other words, although the Church engaged directly in economic enterprises, it did so on a private basis, and not as a part of its functions within the imperial order.

C. The Monopolistic Merchant: The Castilian model imposed upon the American territories necessarily took into account the subjects of the king. Among these, directly linked to the mercantilistic economic structures, were the beneficiaries of royal privilege. Besides the farmers of royal taxes and, in New Spain in particular, the powerful sheep-raisers of the Mesta, we find the powerful merchants of the guilds--the Consulados--created in Mexico and Lima at the turn of the sixteenth century (1592 and 1613, respectively), and established in eight other cities of the empire at the end of the eighteenth. The Consulado, says Haring, was the center in which "the influence of the European residents was anchored":

> [A] center of wealth and conservatism, it served with the rich miners and the Church as the principal source of fluid funds in the community; and in fact, after the abolition of the Cadiz commercial monopoly by the Bourbons, its members were more and more inclined to employ their surplus capital in financing the mining industry.[17]

This closed group of merchants specializing in import-export operated in close connection with the monopolistic merchants of Andalusia. Many of the principal Sevillian houses had agents in the Spanish American cities. The usual pattern, however, was that of partnership contract, inspired by the Italian commenda, both for

---

[16] Ibid.

[17] Ibid., pp. 253-54.

SPANISH BUREAUCRATIC-PATRIMONIALISM IN AMERICA

extraordinary enterprises and for regular commercial relations.

Membership in the <u>Consulados</u> was reserved to peninsular Spaniards. They controlled official trade with Spain and hence the fortunes of the Creole producers. Speculating on shortages of imported goods, they obtained enormous profits. These three factors--their being "<u>chapetones</u>," their control of the international markets, and the role they played in the rise of prices in the local markets--made the <u>Consulados</u> the group which, by virtue of its privileges, stood in the way of development and prosperity, for both producers and consumers. On the eve of Independence, they were the favorite target of Creole attacks and the staunchest partisans of resistance and reaction.

D. <u>The Subject Races</u>: The hierarchical conception of government had to accommodate itself to certain realities, including the native labor force, on which the whole enterprise of colonization was grounded. The Spanish conquest took place at least two centuries before the great demographic expansion of Europe. Potential European emigration--which was, moreover, restricted to Spaniards and, at the beginning, to the subjects of Castile--appeared very weak, especially in comparison to the large aboriginal populations which existed in New Spain and Peru. The natives, whose labor was essential to the sustenance of the small groups of Spaniards, provided the demographic basis for the exploitation of the economic potentialities of the new kingdoms. Once the patrimonial rule was consolidated, the representatives of the Crown did not, in principle, participate directly in the exploitation of local resources by the ruthless mobilization of the available native labor. Rather, their role was to assert the king's proprietary rights both before and after the process of production began.

Insofar as the Crown was concerned, Indians were fitted directly into the patrimonial order, once the theological question of their "human status" was resolved. They paid direct tribute to the king's officials. They were the objects of specific legislation and governed by special agents and special "spiritual guardians." To some extent, at least, the pre-Columbian patterns were respected and, when this obtained, incorporated into the body of legislation. Different ways of integrating the conquered populations into the order of the conquerors were sought, as we shall see hereafter.

The lines of caste that ran across the colonial society were an indication of the principles of social structure used to incorporate the natives into the order brought over from Spain. As Morse writes:

> The Crown considered the political and social hierarchy to be energized at every level and in every department. As

SPANISH BUREAUCRATIC-PATRIMONIALISM AND COLONIAL SOCIETY

Indian peoples were absorbed, for example, they were not indiscriminately reduced to a common denominator. Certain of their leaders retained prestige in the post-conquest society, and many low-born Spaniards raised their own status by marrying caciques' daughters.[18]

The hierarchy was further refined as it began to take into account and to rank differently the ethnic groups that resulted from miscegenation.[19] The *mestizos* (Indian and white mixed-blood) were

---

[18]Morse, "Toward a Theory . . .," p. 55.

[19]Of the term *casta*, applied throughout Spanish America to the "colored" lower class groups, Morse (in "Urbanization in Latin America," *Latin American Research Review*, I, 1, Fall, 1965, p. 41) writes: "Casta does not convey the hermetic, segregative sense of 'caste.' It is more reminiscent of the Thomist-Aristotelian notion of functional social hierarchy. It refers to a 'stratified social group, united by ethnic origin, common juridico-legal status, and a common type of economic-professional occupations and activities.'"
  Quoting from José Gil Fortoul, *Historia Constitucional de Venezuela* (Caracas: Parra Leon Hnos., 1930), Bagú gives the following ethnic divisions in the Western Indies: "Seven castes were distinguished, namely: (1) The Spaniards born in Europe; (2) The Spaniards born in America; (3) The *Mestizos*, descendants of White and Indian; (4) The Mulattoes, descendants of White and Negro; (5) The Zambos, descendants of Indian and Negro; (6) The Indians; (7) The Negroes, with the subdivisions of *Zambo Prieto*, offspring of a Negro and a *Zamba*; *Cuarterones*, offspring of a white man and a mulatto woman; *Quinterones*, of a white man and a *Cuarterona*; and *Salto-Atrás* (or leap backward), the colour of the offspring being, in this case, darker than that of the mother." Bagú adds: "The Laws of the Indies very often refer to the castes, but the terminology and the concepts are vague and contradictory." (*Estructura* . . ., p. 122.)
  The Crown seems to have distrusted deeply the populations resulting from miscegenation. Endowed with greater freedom than the Indians, roaming the countryside as the Argentine *gaucho*, or making a living as best they could in the cities, their place in the "functional social hierarchy" was not clear. They presented, hence, an obvious danger. The awareness of this was expressed in the repeated prohibitions against the carrying of arms by the lower castes "even if they were accompanying their masters" (*ibid*., p. 147). Furthermore, the Crown and the local agents attempted to segregate the vagrant populations from the Indians that were more easily and effectively controlled. Thus, the Royal *Cedula* of the 25th of November of 1578, addressed to the *Audiencia* of Quito, says: "We are informed that it is highly inconvenient for

SPANISH BUREAUCRATIC-PATRIMONIALISM IN AMERICA

considered to be gente de razón (men of reason), one step above the Indians; the latter were the wards of the Crown, so to speak--incapable of taking care of themselves and, as such, the object of the more or less disinterested but always paternalistic attention of the Spanish authorities. At the lower rungs of society we find, after the massive introduction of African slaves, Negroes (whether freed or in bondage), mulattoes, and zambos (Indian-Negro mixed-blood). The position of the "non-white" lower orders was thus fully recognized and established in the hierarchical order of the patrimonial Spanish system. The New Laws that suppressed Indian slavery in 1542, as well as the evolution of the encomienda system, must both be considered as an attempt by the Crown to re-establish its direct domination over the Indian populations, a measure which would tie them more closely to the patrimonial structure of power.[20]

However, "unlike the medieval serf, [Indian and Negro burden-bearers] never fully identified with the historical and cultural ethos of their masters."[21] The point that Morse makes here requires some further comments. By means of their ideological integration into medieval society, the serfs stood in a different position with regard to the feudal lords than did the Indians and Negroes to the producers in Spanish colonial society. The relationship of the former to their masters can be analyzed in terms of what Alain Touraine has called the "constituting conscience" of the serfs.[22] A tradition shared by both rulers and ruled established between them a certain type of symbiotic dependence; by acknowledging the extra-social roots of feudal power, the medieval serfs "constituted" the lords of the land into a ruling warrior class, and committed themselves to a particular form of

---

the good and profit of the native Indians of those provinces that Mulattoes, Mestizos and Negroes be in their company; for, beside treating them ill and using them, they teach them their bad habits and idleness and also some errors and vices which could destroy and impede the fruit we wish for the salvation of the souls of the said Indians, and for their policed life; and because from such company they cannot gain anything whereby they may profit, the said Mulattoes, Negroes and Mestizos being universally so ill-inclined, we command you to prohibit and defend with the utmost care that henceforward they go or be in company of the said Indians or in their countries and villages" (quoted in ibid., p. 147).

[20]For more details, see Appendix.

[21]Morse, "Toward a Theory . . .," p. 57.

[22]Sociologie de l'action (Paris: Seuil, 1965).

SPANISH BUREAUCRATIC-PATRIMONIALISM AND COLONIAL SOCIETY

participation in the system. Domination by a warrior class is essential in a feudal society, which lacks, on the whole, "internal" means of generalized economic growth. Expansion depends largely upon violence and conquest, and plunder of external units becomes an important factor in growth. Violence, managed by the class of warriors, serves thus a "positive" purpose for each "closed" unit of the system.

The analogy with feudalism--which has often been made with reference to the relations between the latifundista and his dependents--cannot be pushed very far in the case of Spanish America. On the one hand, the economic system was not, as a rule, "closed," but rather oriented toward trade (and particularly international trade) from the beginning. On the other hand, violence was aimed mainly at transforming the indigenous populations into a labor force which would ensure the subsistence of the relatively small groups of conquerors and colonists. Their incorporation into the system took different forms in the colonial context and was not, in our opinion, comparable to the ideally "integrated" feudal situation.

Where the Indian tribes came directly under the power of the patrimonial king, their patterns of life were respected and their rights to the land, on the whole, guaranteed. The Crown superimposed a patrimonial bond, required the presence of a priest (in accordance with its mission of evangelization), and exacted from its new subjects the tribute due to the patrimonial lord. The local representatives of the patrimonial power--often with the help of the Indian caciques--generally profited by their position and subjected the Indian communities to the most blatant abuses. However, as proved by the many Indian revolts against local authorities, the integration of the Indians into the Spanish system was, at one level, achieved. The famous uprising of Tupac Amaru in Peru, for instance, was led "against bad government, in the name of the King."[23] Simultaneously, in this case, as in many others, reference was made to a basis of claim that was external to the patrimonial system--namely, the past of the Indian peoples and the defense of their autonomy and community organizations. Appealing to the Crown on the basis of their specific identity and their pre-conquest status, the Indians, in this case, were included in the patrimonial structure as a distinct social group.[24]

---

[23]See Appendix, p. 118.

[24]The Indians that were under ecclesiastic administration do not constitute a special case except for the segregated "Jesuitic theocracies" of Paraguay. After the fathers were forced out, the settlements declined and gradually disappeared. Many of the missionary Indians, once the "theocratic" bond (or Jesuit force) was

SPANISH BUREAUCRATIC-PATRIMONIALISM IN AMERICA

The wars of independence provide an indirect illustration of the different relations existing between the Indians and the Crown, on the one hand, and, on the other hand, between the local oligarchies and the "subject race"; while the Crown in its resistance to the secessionists could draw very largely on the Indian populations, especially in Peru, the Creole groups did not, on the whole, show much confidence in the Indians. It could even be argued (particularly in the cases of Mexico and Peru) that the Indian uprisings represented a threat to the Creole elites, and that this potential danger, where it existed, fostered the internal cohesion of the oligarchic groups after Independence.

The post-Independence governments provided the Indians living on large estates and tilling their own small plots with a protection even weaker and more ineffective than that of the Spanish Crown, and there was no longer a superior power to whom--or in the name of which--they might appeal. However attached they were to the landowners by force, indebtedness, tradition, or, above all, lack of other possibilities, they still waged sporadic revolts against abuse (ruthless exploitation, in fact, which alternated with paternalism) in the name of their communal identity and their lost autonomy. But where detribalization occurred, the Indians--and, after 1518, the increasing numbers of African slaves --became a servile labor force, uprooted, herded like cattle, and ruthlessly exploited in mines and large-scale plantations. Revolts, if they took place at all, could not make an appeal there to traditional safeguards nor to the cultural identity of a now subject race. The pattern was one of accidental and savage uprisings in response to intolerable hardship, or, as was frequent among Negroes on commercial plantations, one of escape and foundation of independent communities in wild and remote areas.[25]

---

eliminated, reverted to their primitive forms of communal organization and went back to the forests. This would prove that the basic pattern of Indian life, however primitive, had not been essentially altered by the Jesuitic rule, except for the fragile evangelization. (On the contrary, as a rule the Jesuits strove to preserve the language and the original crafts of the natives.) Many other Indians passed under the brutal rule of military administrators and finally deserted. Others still were absorbed into the laboring groups of other regions of the viceroyalty of the Rio de la Plata, entering thus different relations of dependency and meeting the fate common to the Indians of Spanish America after Independence.

[25] Bagú, *Estructura* . . . . For historical details on the recurrence of violence and revolt (or massive escape of the servile labor force), see Chap. IV: "Class Conflict."

SPANISH BUREAUCRATIC-PATRIMONIALISM AND COLONIAL SOCIETY

Though the type of domination they encountered might vary, the "subject races" (except for those Indian tribes who retreated to the highlands or otherwise remained marginal to the economic system of the colonies) became the laboring basis of society. It is not surprising, therefore, that manual work would be considered a symbol of servility in Spanish America--a symbol further embedded by its association with race and caste lines.

There were, it is true, groups of white craftsmen, retail merchants, and small independent farmers. The Crown had made repeated efforts to encourage the emigration of the Spanish "working-classes."

As these colonists of the laboring class were inclined to desert their trades and secure an allotment of Indians, the Crown ordered in 1508 that they be compelled to work at their accustomed occupations. In 1511, the king was urging the Casa de Contratación to send out as many farm laborers as possible, to simplify the formalities at Seville, and to advertise throughout the poorer regions of Castile the richness of the islands and the opportunities for improving one's lot by emigration. . . . [I]n 1518, . . . farmers who would go to Hispaniola or Tierra firme were promised passage and maintenance from the day they arrived in Seville until they disembarked in America, besides lands, implements, seeds, livestock, and living for a year, the services of a physician and apothecary, relief from taxes, and premiums for the best husbandry. Concessions such as these were repeated in later years.[26]

However, the pattern that the colonists tried to follow was different; they had come to the New World to achieve the status and fortune they did not have in Spain. The main sources of wealth, and, hence, of social power, derived, in a mercantilistic economic system, from production for the market. This, in turn, depended on the control they could secure over land, mines, and labor forces. Although the colonists engaged in the exploitation of the American resources were indispensable to the task of colonization, their tendency to establish autonomous rights upon the king's patrimony distinguished them from bureaucrats, clergymen, and burden-bearers: they represented the "centrifugal forces" with which every patrimonial monarchy has to reckon. Where their original projects failed, or could not even be attempted, the Spanish immigrants or descendants remained in the towns, in those occupational groups generically classified by Bagú as "colonial middle classes." Thus, they reinforced the basic pattern of an urban-centered enterprise of colonization.

---

[26] Haring, op. cit., pp. 206-7.

SPANISH BUREAUCRATIC-PATRIMONIALISM IN AMERICA

THE RELATIONSHIPS BETWEEN THE "CENTRIFUGAL FORCES" AND THE SPANISH ORDER

The reestablishment of royal control over the small groups of early conquistadors and their descendants was marked by one bloody uprising after another. The most significant was perhaps that of the Peruvian encomenderos and vecinos, under the command of Gonzalo Pizarro, against the king's representatives. The viceroy Núñez de Vela, who arrived in 1544 with the mandate of enforcing the New Laws, could read the following inscription on a wall of Lima: "El que me quisiere quitar los esclavos y pueblos que tengo en encomienda por S.M. mire lo que hace, quiza podra ser que primero lo eche de la tierra o le quite la vida."[27] The revolt of the colonists went even further and directly challenged the king's authority (not only that of his delegates), as evidenced by the separatist claims of Francisco de Carbajal and the letter written by Lope de Aguirre to Philip II after Lope had proclaimed a king of Peru, Tierra Firme, and Chile: "Mira, mira, rey español, que no sea cruel a tus vasallos ni ingrato, pues estando tu padre y tú en los reinos de Espana sin ninguna zozobra, te han dado tus vasallos a costa de su sangre y haciendo tantos reinos y señoríos como en estas partes tienes."[28]

The claims of the rebels were founded on their "rightful" expectations of patrimonial rewards and grants, owed to them by the king in whose name they had conquered and occupied the newfound lands. When the viceroy Pedro de la Gasca of Peru abrogated the decree abolishing the encomiendas, the rebels gradually rallied to the Crown, which bestowed new repartimientos, plots of land, offices, and rewards. In later years, the great viceroy Francisco de Toledo tried to impress upon the king the necessity of a strong, albeit subordinate, class of landowners. Arguing in favor of perpetual encomiendas, he reflected both the "feudalistic" tendency of the Creoles and the difficulties he encountered when trying to obtain military service from the encomenderos and vecinos. Assured by the Crown of their economic and social power,

---

[27]Quoted by Jorge Basadre in La Multitud, la ciudad y el campo en la historia del Peru (2a. ed.; Lima: Huascaran, 1947), p. 46. Translation: "He who would take away from me the slaves and villages that I have in encomienda by H.M., he better watch what he does, it might be that before I will throw him out of this land or take his life." [My translation.]

[28]Ibid., p. 53. Translation: "Watch, watch, Spanish king, do not be cruel to your vassals or ungrateful, for, while your father and you were in the kingdoms of Spain without any trouble, your vassals have given you, at the expense of their blood and doings, as many kingdoms and lordships as you hold in these lands."

the latter would become the natural defenders of the order. Experience in other countries had revealed the usefulness of "cabezas con asiento y perpetuidad de mayorazgos o feudos unidos y dependientes del Rey y de otras personas obligadas a su Rey por mercedes y privilegios y gajes, los cuales todos, cuando se ofreciere alguna alteración tengan por propia la causa de defensa y conservación del reino en obediencia de su Rey."[29] At the same time, the Padre Bivero insisted:

> Es necesario que Vuestra Magestad dé orden con brevedad para que en cada pueblo de españoles de este reino haya por lo menos una docena de hombres que tengan feudo perpetuo y suficiente, en la caja de Vuestra Magestad o donde mejor pareciere, para que sean nervios de la Republica y puedan en paz y en guerra sustentarla, porque do otra manera se va acabando a mas andar.[30]

However, in spite of the privileges (such as the right of entailment for the great estates) that the Crown granted or could not curb, the general pattern was absolutistic. Jealous of its power, the Crown never conceded jurisdictional prerogatives to the *encomenderos*, in spite of their demands. The *encomienda* never became a fief, but remained a source of personal services and tributes.

What distrust the king showed with regard to his own agents was obviously multiplied with respect to the Creole elites. Having experienced very early the dangers of the entrenchment of privileges, and the difficulties, if not the impossibility, of attaining effective control, the Crown followed the policy of excluding systematically its most powerful subjects from active participation in the political and juridical organization of the Indies. As Bagú has written, the general norm was "no group too powerful, and

---

[29] Quoted by Bagú in *Estructura* . . ., pp. 161-62. Translation: "heads with stability and perpetuity of *mayorazgos* or 'fiefs' united and dependent upon the king and of other persons obliged to their king by mercies and privileges and grants [so that] all of them, should some change occur, make their own the cause of the defense and conservation of the kingdom in obedience of their king."

[30] "It is necessary that Your Majesty orders shortly that in each town of Spaniards of this kingdom there be at least a dozen men with a perpetual and sufficient 'fief,' either in Your Majesty's own patrimony or where it may seem better, so that they may be nerves of the Republic and may sustain it in peace or in war, because otherwise it goes toward its end as the time passes." Quoted by Bagú in *ibid*.

SPANISH BUREAUCRATIC-PATRIMONIALISM IN AMERICA

all of them subordinate to the imperial power."[31] The social policy of the empire thus became oriented by the purpose "of neatly delimiting the range of each class [or groups of population, differing in terms of rights and economic power], . . . of indicating, even in its details, in what forms and circumstances the subordination that all groups owe to the Crown should be manifested."[32] On the one hand, the Crown was well aware that it could not control effectively the social power derived from wealth, if for no other reason than that the pioneering economic enterprise could not (given the material and ideological conditions at the time of the conquest and colonization) be centrally directed by the state. The economic exploitation of the newfound lands necessarily had to be entrusted to private enterprise. The most that could be done--and in this the Spanish imperial achievement is remarkable --was to superimpose regulations on the system of production, to control access to the means of production, and place a toll on the results. But, on the other hand, the Crown <u>could</u> attempt to monopolize power in the political and juridical spheres directly created by its action. We thus arrive at the following proposition: <u>The Spanish version of arbitrary patrimonialism, autocratic in the political sphere, could not totally reduce the autonomy in the socio-economic sphere. The particular lines of conflict in the socio-economic sphere derived from a general conflict between the Castilian political model and the "centrifugal" forces of society</u>. It is in this light that we can approach the antagonism between Creoles and Spaniards--the former representing "autonomous" economic and social forces, the latter traditionally privileged positions.

Legally, the status of Spaniards and Creoles was the same. "Indeed, the Crown repeatedly instructed viceroys and presidents that in filling vacancies preference be given to properly qualified men born in the Indies, especially to descendants of the conquistadores and other early settlers."[33] In practice, the appointments made in Spain (and appointments were for the most part made there, as we know) were bestowed upon peninsular Spaniards. The meager opportunities that the Creoles had within the official hierarchies (both lay and ecclesiastic) were still more circumscribed with the greater centralization of control under the Bourbons. Thus,

> Creoles were generally excluded from places of responsibility and authority. They were represented in the <u>cabildos</u>, to a

---

[31]<u>Ibid</u>., p. 170.

[32]<u>Ibid</u>., p. 160.

[33]Haring, <u>op. cit</u>., pp. 194-95.

SPANISH BUREAUCRATIC-PATRIMONIALISM AND COLONIAL SOCIETY

slight extent in the ecclesiastical hierarchy, and more frequently in minor administrative posts such as that of corregidor [eliminated by the intendentes reform in the 1780's]. Very occasionally a Creole rose to the rank of oidor in one of the colonial audiencias, or was appointed to a post in the royal exchequer. But in such cases the appointment was made in a colony other than that of which the Creole official was a native.[34]

The special jurisdictions--endowed with strong privileges within the patrimonial and mercantilist structure--strove to monopolize these privileges and exclude the Creoles. Thus, the Consulado, in 1729, "prohibited Creole merchants in America from serving as agents. . . . This order was rescinded in 1738, but Creoles were still permitted to do business at Cadiz only through Spanish merchants matriculated in the Indies trade."[35]

As Baron von Humboldt wrote at the end of the eighteenth century, social distance was added to the exclusion from the higher spheres of colonial officialdom: "The most miserable European, without education, and without intellectual cultivation, thinks himself superior to the whites born in the new continent."[36] In spite of their social and political inferiority to the metropolitan Spaniards, the Creoles were not a homogeneous group. Subjects of the patrimonial king, they were included in the detailed hierarchy of society and, as such, related to the Spanish order by different degrees of privilege. Thus, if we take a broad view of the colonial society, we find, at first sight, two differentiating cultural elements. The taint placed by the Spanish system on manual and commercial activities as well as the social value conferred on the ownership of land downgraded the status of the groups of Creole merchants and professionals. Obviously, the rank of those whom Bagú has called the "colonial middle-classes" (the small landholders, the professionals inseparable from urban life, the salaried managers of the great estates, the petty officers connected with the government and the Church) was even lower.

Between the various groups of Creoles and the Indian or

---

[34] Ibid., p. 302.

[35] Ibid.

[36] Alexander von Humboldt, Political Essay on the Kingdom of New Spain, reprinted under the title "Creoles or Americans" [excerpts from Vol. I, pp. 204-6, 209-11, English edition, trans. and ed. by John Black (London, 1811)] in R. A. Humphreys and J. Lynch, eds., The Origins of the Latin American Revolutions (New York: A. Knopf, 1965), p. 270.

Negro laborers, there was another, lower class, not sharply differentiated from the colored labor force. This class consisted of the unemployed masses who plagued the cities and the neighboring countryside. Mixed-bloods who refused to become part of the servile labor force, permanent or temporary unemployed, retainers of some important vecino, or, simply, déclassés, vagrants, and delinquents--all these groups formed, so to speak, an "interstitial" population. These unbound groups, whether urban or rural, often provided a "masse de manoeuvre" for the urban riots and the wars of independence.

The internal differentiation of the groups of American-born whites can be clearly grasped if we focus the discussion on their differing relationships to the colonial economic system. Thus, the qualification of "interstitial" that we applied to the urban and rural "unattached" or unemployed is justified by their marginality with regard to the predominant economic structures. On the other hand, the groups of Creole "possessors"--landowners, miners, and merchants--and the "colonial middle classes," though they were politically and socially subordinate to the Spanish-born groups, nonetheless found a place within the order. The propertied groups--the Creole elites--geared their economic activities toward the mercantilistic imperial system, and their activity was meaningful within that framework. But as Spain's economic and financial power was increasingly challenged by other European countries, this same framework was seen as intolerably restrictive.[37]

The economic system of imperial Spain, geared as it was toward the accumulation of money for the treasury, provided the structure within which the first settlers and their descendants went to seek their fortunes. The main sources of wealth were those products--gold and silver first of all, then sugar (as in the Antilles and Peru), cacao (as in Venezuela), leather (as in Mexico and, above all, Argentina), etc.--that could advantageously be placed on the European markets. Inevitably, as Spain decayed and entered a phase of stagnation, its monopoly on trade was increasingly resented within the developing colonial economies. (This point will be reconsidered later in the discussion of the main determinants of the independence movements.)

From what has been said thus far, we can assert this general proposition about economic power in the colonies: Control

---

[37] By 1700 the monopolistic Spanish merchants had become mere intermediates between the developing European economies and the Indies: foreign countries supplied 5/6 of the manufactures consumed in Spain, 9/10 of the American trade (Haring, op. cit., p. 295).

SPANISH BUREAUCRATIC-PATRIMONIALISM AND COLONIAL SOCIETY

of the factors of production (a cheap labor force available for exploitation, and land or mining concessions), combined with a rising European demand for the staples produced, determined the relative importance of the various oligarchic groups, and, at the same time, the changes in their fortunes.

Thus, if we take the greater or lesser availability of labor as a factor which determined the differences in economic power of the various Creole elites, the colonists of the Rio de la Plata compared very poorly with the "aristocracies" of New Spain, New Granada, and Peru. In one case, the settlers could avail themselves of the labor of sedentary Indian tribes--and, later, of African slaves--while, in the other, there was no such labor supply and the settlers were forced to pit their meager forces against the incursions of warlike and primitive pampas Indians. Bagú, considering jointly two of the factors of economic power mentioned by us, describes in the following manner the economic "inferiority" of the Rio de la Plata elites:

> In Mexico and Peru, the latifundia grew at the expense of Indian property. . . . In the Rio de la Plata, on the contrary, powerful and influential oligarchies did not emerge, as in the other colonies--because there was not in the region a labor force sufficient to exploit those enormous latifundia --even if there had been one, the latifundistas would not have been able to extract from their land the products that the international market demanded most and that were provided by other American regions--ore, diamonds, sugar, tobacco, cacao, cotton. They would have to wait until the last years of the nineteenth century to place on the market a staple that would permit the formation of a powerful oligarchy, i.e., bovine meat.[38]

In fact, at the end of the eighteenth century, the most prosperous parts of the viceroyalty of the Rio de la Plata were the provinces of the interior (even though their decay was foreordained in the eighteenth century by the opening of Buenos Aires to international commerce). Unlike the warrior tribes of the pampas, the Indians of the northwest and center of the Rio de la Plata had been subdued as early as the sixteenth century.[39] Furthermore, these

---

[38] Bagú, Estructura . . ., pp. 76-77.

[39] Aldo Ferrer, Las Etapas de la economía Argentina (Mexico y Buenos Aires: FCE, 1963), Chap. I. In the sixteenth century, 20,000 Indians had already been given in encomienda in Mendoza, 12,000 in Córdoba, and the same number in Santiago del Estero. In the Northwest, around 1650, 30,000 to 40,000 Indians were encomendados.

provinces were linked to the markets of Alto Peru. Even though they did not participate directly in the only dynamic sector of the colonial economy--that is, foreign trade--this linkage explains the development of consumer industries and agricultural activities (cotton raising, textile manufacture, cattle raising, and, in particular, the supplying of mules for the Potosi mines, the production of wine in Mendoza and San Juan, etc.). This example illustrates a point previously made: the significance of economic activities (and hence the social power of the groups who controlled them) depended on the possibilities of exportation of their products to markets large enough to make the activities profitable.

Wealth and the social influence thus derived were chiefly concentrated in the hands of small groups who had access to commercial circuits, whether inter-regional or international. The existence and activities of these groups created, in turn, the most substantial part of internal demand. This demand--which could have diversified the economy and opened new channels of social mobility for the local groups--was limited for several reasons. Because the level of technology was very low, the dynamic sectors of the economy engendered only negligible "induction effects." Based as it was on large amounts of cheap labor, the development of these sectors could have stimulated local economies. However, what occurred in the Argentine Northwest, for instance, was just the reverse: the Indian labor force was constantly diverted toward the mines of Alto Peru, with a consequent crisis in the local industries.[40] (Another example is the transfer of Chilean Indians to the mining sectors of Peru.) The material needs of the labor force remained at a subsistence level. Thus, the demand created in the local markets was only for very low-priced commodities.[41]

Therefore, the groups which could have served as a source of substantial demand for local manufactures remained extremely small: they were limited, in fact, to the wealthy few occupying one end of the polarized system of colonial social stratification. Despite the Creole origin of these groups, their patterns of consumption were inspired by Spain and oriented toward European products. Spain's monopoly certainly accentuated, if not directly caused, these intertwined factors of distortion:

> Spain did not uniformly require the colonists to take the commodities [it provided] in preference to the products of

---

[40]Bagú, Estructura . . ., pp. 84-85.

[41]The early development of the Argentine meat industry was based on the exportation of beef jerky to the slave plantations of Brazil and the Antilles.

their own manufacture. . . . Interference by the metropolis with colonial industry . . . was never very systematic. . . . Occasionally, attempts were made to suppress a colonial industry [as, for instance, in the case of Peruvian vineyards and olive plantations], either in the interests of peninsular trade or to protect native labor from exploitation, but it was rarely possible to enforce the decrees in their entirety.[42]

Spain, stubbornly defending its privileges and its central position in the system of American trade, discouraged, if not prohibited, any attempts at large-scale inter-colonial commerce. Such commerce could probably have provided a solid basis for the economic activities not primarily oriented toward the peninsular market, and thus increased the possibilities of mobility in the social stratification scale.

In *Estructura social de la colonia,* Bagú has pointed out the particular instability of the "middle groups." Unprotected by the Crown, they did not have access to the main factors of production--land, the servile labor force, or even capital. They remained in the dependency of the wealthier Creoles and tied to their fortunes. The local crafts, moreover, depended upon a rigid guild system organized along the classic European pattern. The regulations of the guilds--generally issued by the cabildos and sanctioned by the viceroy--were anachronistic and antiquated. Although their retarding effect upon the growth of local industries was already recognized at the beginning of the eighteenth century, the rigid ranking and system of promotion (as well as the regulation of quality, prices, and competition--and some rudiments of protection of the workers) persisted until a late period.[43] Thus, if a craftsman was a member of a guild, he could eventually have access to the group of masters or employers who controlled the industry. If, however, he was excluded from the higher ranks of the guild system--as was the case for Indians (whose skills were feared as a dangerous potential competition), for Negroes, for mulattoes, and, in some cases, for mestizos--he was hopelessly debarred from the most profitable aspects of his trade.

The Creole economic elites, as we have pointed out in the previous examples, were also subject to the particular hazards of the hybrid system of colonial capitalism, with its monopolistic control over exportable products, and, more generally, to the oscillations of the peninsular market. Indeed, some of the most

---

[42] Haring, op. cit., pp. 242-43.

[43] In Mexico, for instance, the guild system was not abolished until 1861.

SPANISH BUREAUCRATIC-PATRIMONIALISM IN AMERICA

successful groups during the eighteenth century operated on the fringes of the economy, in an area opened by the imperfections of the monopolistic system. Such groups were engaged, in particular, in the ever-growing contraband trade, centered chiefly in Buenos Aires, Chile, and the Antilles, and, despite widespread venality and corruption, lived a semi-legal economic existence.

Up to now, we have stressed the relationships between the colonial "propertied groups" and the market on which their fortunes depended. Under the mercantilistic system and the arbitrary patrimonialism of the Crown, there was a distinction between a precarious economic elite (whose wealth was tied to local markets) and the most powerful groups--whether merchants or large-scale producers of colonial staples--who were more closely related to the "central" spheres of colonial economic activity. This distinction does not take into account the "aristocracies" whose privileges originated in the first phase of the conquest. To suggest the significance of this group in later years, we have to consider specifically the factor that is generally regarded as the most important determinant of social stratification in Spanish America --namely, the possession of land.

In theory, social recognition in the colonies derived mainly from landed property. Land determined social prestige. Furthermore, it conferred on the land-owning Creoles the possibility of exercising the few political rights that the absolutistic Spanish system allowed them to enjoy. "Since 1503," writes Haring, "Castilian law allowed any subject above the rank of peasant to erect his property, real or personal, into a mayorazgo with the title of Don, which forbade his entering any profession attached to commerce or industry on pain of loss of status."[44] This, joined with the exploitation of a semi-servile labor force, and the conception of work typical of the caste ordering of society, has led many writers to stress the feudal features of Latin America. Thus, Jacques Lambert has maintained that the encomienda "delegates a part of the sovereign's power to private individuals . . . and creates personal relations between masters and dependents." As such, it becomes, he says, the first element of a feudal order, later indicated by "the linking of the personal power of the encomendero with the property of the large estate."[45] In some cases, it is true, the "hacienda" system to which Lambert alludes may have developed on the basis of an encomienda. Or rights upon the land and control of workers may have been established together from the start. (Morse suggests that this would point to the estancia form.) However, the specific nature and the

---

[44] Op. cit., p. 198.

[45] Amérique Latine (Paris: PUF, 1963), Chap. III. [My translation

58

SPANISH BUREAUCRATIC-PATRIMONIALISM AND COLONIAL SOCIETY

evolution of the encomienda are not adequately taken into account in the above argument. As pointed out by Morse, among others, the encomienda was not a grant of land, but "the entrusting of a community of Indians to a Spanish colonist who collected from them various forms of tribute and was obliged to protect them and assist their assimilation into Christian civilization."[46] In the sixteenth century, by a special royal decree, the encomenderos and their families were forbidden to reside on the territory of the encomienda. "An encomendero," says Morse, "had only limited rights to acquire holdings within his encomienda, and these were not to encroach upon Indian community lands. The encomienda further differed from a land grant in that: (1) it was a grant for a limited number of lives and not a permanent alienation; (2) it was a grant conferred by the Crown and not locally."[47] As we have seen before, even in the first phase in which the encomiendas were granted as a reward for services rendered, the bond between king and conquistadors was not feudalistic but patrimonial.

In the words of Mario Góngora, "the specifically vassalic relation of loyalty is overshadowed by the general loyalty of subjects to the king; the link between conquistadors and king assumes a new aspect, not through a personal bond distinct from what they have as subjects, but through the relations which they have with the lands won for the royal domain."[48] The hostility shown by the Crown against possible feudal entrenchments was manifest in the arbitrariness with which the encomiendas were revoked and redistributed until the final suppression in the years 1718 to 1721. As pointed out by Bagú, this was a powerful instrument by means of which the Crown changed at will the physiognomy of many local oligarchies.[49] However, at the time when the institution disappeared, the encomiendas were not as desirable as they had been, chiefly because of the heavier and heavier royal taxes that weighed on them. At that period, says Morse, a landed elite had already come into being by other means. This was the "colonial Creole aristocracy . . . often of humble or socially marginal origins. . . . It had extensive social power, especially in the regions distant from the viceregal capitals of New Spain and Peru, al-

---

[46] Morse, "The Heritage of Latin America," in Louis Hartz, ed., The Founding of New Societies (New York: Harcourt, Brace & World, Inc., 1964), pp. 148-50.

[47] Ibid.

[48] El Estado en el derecho indiano: epoca de fundación (1492-1570) (Santiago de Chile: Instituto de Investigaciones Histórico-Culturales, Universidad de Chile, 1951), pp. 184-85 in particular. [My translation.]

[49] Bagú, Estructura . . ., p. 83.

though its political participation was generally limited to town government."[50] It thrived on the basis of municipal land grants (the cabildos, until 1754, had the power to attribute land to the town's vecinos); it asserted de facto rights to vacant lands or grabbed them from the commons and the Indian holdings, or it simply invested revenues from other sources in land.[51]

The hacienda system, typical of the nineteenth century and even of many Latin American areas today, arose in this way. Aided by isolation and dispersion, as well as by their influence on local political agencies, the landowners found in their estates the de facto autonomy which, for Weber, orients the action of "centrifugal forces" in centralized patrimonial states. The workers of the hacienda--generally Indians who maintained certain forms of community life--had access but no right to the land. They fell under the hacendado's more or less paternalistic jurisdiction, and were kept in bondage through the system of peonaje (quasi-forced labor based on systematic and chronic indebtedness). These local patrimonies contrasted with the capitalistic plantations producing one main staple for the market with slave labor, or later, with hired workhands. The differences between the latter, economically "progressive" and the former, economically unproductive agricultural structures were accentuated by the nineteenth-century period of economic growth.

The above considerations are evidence of the generally recognized social value of land, and support the assertion of Jacques Lambert who, referring to the economic potentialities of the early eighteenth century, writes: "The land of Latin America became private property before it could actually be exploited."[52] However, at least in colonial times, the existence of a closed land-based oligarchy seems questionable. In a mercantilistic system stressing the accumulation of money, and in a social context where urban life was always very important, wealth became the necessary determinant of status and social mobility, however limited the access to the sources of wealth may have been. As we said before, land could always be bought, conquered in the wilderness, or usurped from the Indian communities. (The latter two practices, in fact, prevailed during the nineteenth century, when

---

[50] "The Heritage . . .," p. 147.

[51] The Crown was interested in reasserting its patrimonial rights at a time when land values rose, as is proved by its "intermittent warfare against improper land titles." The outcome of this was a decree which, in 1754, authorized the audiencias to decide on matters of proerty titles and to attribute land grants.

[52] Op. cit.

SPANISH BUREAUCRATIC-PATRIMONIALISM AND COLONIAL SOCIETY

the Crown's protection of the Indians was lifted and the conquest of the territory completed.) In the relatively static colonial societies, moreover, investments were made more for acquiring status than for entrepreneurial ventures. Besides the distinction conferred by owning land, other social distinctions were directly accessible to the rich Creoles, regardless of their lineage. Thus, the positions in the cabildos could very early be bought by almost anyone, after Philip II generalized the practice of selling offices. Similarly, the hidalguías

> could always be obtained from the Crown for a price, often with dispensation from the quality of mestizo. In 1557, Philip II, to meet his pressing financial necessities, ordered one thousand hidalguías sold to persons of all classes without question of defect of lineage, and later sovereigns followed the same practice. Every Creole, therefore, who acquired a fortune sought to buy a title or decoration and to create a mayorazgo. In Lima, in the XVIIIth century there were over forty families of Counts and Marquises.[53]

If anything, the decline of the traditional encomendero aristocracy opened the way to new groups and made possible the emergence of small but powerful oligarchies whose wealth came from various sources (a theme reconsidered in today's Peru by François Bourricaud).[54] As early as the seventeenth century, Padre Cobo, writing about Lima, gave evidence of the mixed origins of economic power: "The wealth of the most part," he says, "consists of money and real estate, such as legacies, orchards, vineyards, sugar mills, textile manufactures, cattle estancias, possession and revenues from mayorazgos and encomiendas of Indians."[55] The ascension of the new social groups in Chile which based their status on money is described by Alberto Edwards:

> Since well before 1810, the ancient families of conquistadores and encomenderos, ruined by luxury and idleness, or extinguished in war or in the cloister, were in complete decadence. The new lineages of merchants and working men--who only had three or four generations of affluence and social status--had slowly come to absorb them and take their place. Thus a mixed aristocracy, of bourgeois origins, came to dominate the country, owing to the triumph of money and by means of its entrepreneurial and mercantilistic spirit;

---

[53]Haring, op. cit., p. 198.

[54]"Remarques sur l'oligarchie péruvienne," Revue française de science politique, Vol. XIV, 4, August, 1964.

[55]Quoted in Bagú, Estructura . . . .

SPANISH BUREAUCRATIC-PATRIMONIALISM IN AMERICA

it was sensible and parsimonious, of regular and orderly habits, but through its veins also ran the blood of some of the old feudal families.[56]

Hence, it could be said that there was, surprisingly enough, a relative openness in the higher rungs of Creole society. What were relatively closed, in the colonial framework, were the alternative sources of wealth by means of which access to the status symbols of the traditional elites could be gained. This suggests both an oligarchic trend and a context in which the cultural values of the aristocracy were more stable than its economic basis. In other words, where economic change was slow and, above all, uncertain, traditional criteria prevailed in the determination of prestige and status. We shall come back later to some of the consequences implied by the possibilities of social mobility at the top of the indigenous social hierarchy.

The American territories did not have, within the Spanish imperial system, the status of colonies, but that of kingdoms, dynastically attached to the Crown and, in principle, equal to the various kingdoms of the mother country. However, although the linkages of the traditional colonial aristocracies with the local representatives of the Spanish order may have been very close in certain cases, the Creole elites were nonetheless socially, politically, and economically subordinate to the Spaniards. Excluded from the most profitable business activities by the powerful and conservative Consulados, maintained in subordinate positions in the colonial and metropolitan regiments, suffering from the restrictions and the exactions imposed by the arbitrary financial policies of the Crown, and politically unrepresented, the Creole elites were bound to become estranged from the colonial order. In fact, resentment against Spain and the desire to maintain their distance with respect to the colored castas were probably the most important (if not the sole) factors of cohesion among the heterogeneous Creole groups. As contacts increased with other parts of the world, the Spanish system--and, in particular, its economic and financial policies--came increasingly to be seen in the light of its more restrictive and paralyzing aspects.

Prosperity and improved administration could only intensify the growing aspirations of the Creoles. This, of course, is a well-known story. Control was not so perfect under the Spanish rule that lines of conflict could not be foreseen before they came into the open with the struggles for independence. However subordinate and directly or indirectly dependent on the mercantilistic and patrimonial structures of the empire, the local elites

---

[56]La fronda aristocrática (Santiago de Chile: Imprenta Nacional, 1928), p. 9.

SPANISH BUREAUCRATIC-PATRIMONIALISM AND COLONIAL SOCIETY

within the colonial order were still guaranteed a certain degree of social autonomy. But would this autonomy lead to the emergence of an elite sufficiently powerful to challenge the Spanish order? The latter was remarkably far-reaching in spite of its ambiguities, and it had prevailed for more than three centuries. Thus, we can assume that, to reorganize society along radically different lines, it would take a total "revolutionary" project buttressed by powerful social forces. To discuss this point adequately requires an analysis of the colonial elites in relation to the "urban phenomenon."

IV

PATTERNS OF URBANIZATION AND URBAN ATTITUDES:
THE BREAKDOWNS OF THE MODEL

THE URBAN PHENOMENON AS AN EXPRESSION OF THE POLITICAL ORDER

From its earliest days, the colonization of Spanish America was urban-centered. The first acts of the small groups of conquistadors and early settlers in the new continent were the foundation of towns from which penetration and conquest of the territory could be undertaken. The Spanish colonial town, writes Haring,

> generally had an individual founder who . . . went about his undertaking as one would fix the location of a manufacturing establishment. He selected the town size, indicated the place for the central plaza, the church and the town hall, marked out the street plan, distributed the lots and gave the future city a name. All of those present who were to become members of the municipality signed the act of organization and took an oath to support it. The founder then appointed a town council and magistrates, and, before this body himself, swore to maintain it.[1]

The political structure embodied in the act of foundation in Latin America preceded the economic function which, in Europe, placed most towns at the center of inter-regional or international commercial networks. Therefore, Basadre, contrasting the Spanish American towns with their European counterparts, stresses their "artificial" character.[2] If, however, the American towns are compared with the Spanish rather than with the northern European municipalities, the similarities appear to be more striking than the differences.[3]

---

[1]C. H. Haring, The Spanish Empire in America (New York: Harcourt, Brace & World, Inc., 1963), p. 149.

[2]Jorge Basadre, La Multitud, la ciudad y el campo en la historia del Perú (2a. ed.; Lima: Huascaran, 1947).

[3]See Mario Góngora, El Estado en el derecho indiano: epoca de fundación (1492-1570) (Santiago de Chile: Instituto de Investigaciones Histórico-Culturales, Universidad de Chile, 1951), pp. 180-81. See also R. Morse, "Some Characteristics of Latin American Urban History," American Historical Review, LXVII, 2, January, 1962, pp. 335-36.

PATTERNS OF URBANIZATION AND URBAN ATTITUDES

Whatever the similarities with the Spanish Reconquest of Spain from the Moors, the conquest of America took place in the deserted and "open" setting of the New World. This fact had a bearing, in the first place, on the conformation of the new towns. After the first years, in which the plans "seem to have flowed from medieval practice and to have showed . . . occasional Indian influences,"[4] the towns followed an ideal pattern that had never been so perfectly achieved in the age-old communal structures of peninsular Spain. The first royal instructions on urban planning, brought to America in 1514 by Pedrarias Davila, recommended:

> [L]et the city lots be regular from the start, so that once they are marked out the town will appear well ordered as to the place which is left for a plaza, the site for the church and the sequence of the streets; for in places newly established, proper order can be given from the start, and thus they remain ordered with no extra labor or cost; otherwise order will never be introduced.[5]

The master plan may have come to reflect later the rational transformation of urban complexes noted by Lewis Mumford as part of the rise of "baroque" power. Says Morse:

> Whether or not the Renaissance left its clear mark upon the disposition and construction of the civic center, the decisive feature of the master grid was the subordination of the streets to a central will. That is, the streets cease to be lines of centripetal forces which create the plaza by their confluence; on the contrary, they radiate to the limit of the motive power of the organism of the city, now become aggressive in space.[6]

In the plaza was the vertex of the town, and around it, facing each other, were the symbols of the conquest: the power of the king in its legislative and repressive aspects, and the spiritual foundation of that power embodied in the presence of the church.

The above considerations show the relationships between the conformation of the Spanish American town and both its political origin and its main function. They are further evidenced by Basadre's description:

> The cities were usually surrounded by inalienable commons.

---

[4] Ibid., p. 319.

[5] Quoted by Morse, loc. cit.

[6] Ibid., pp. 320-21.

SPANISH BUREAUCRATIC-PATRIMONIALISM IN AMERICA

... The importance of the plots conceded in the city itself derived from their proximity to the central plaza. The city was placed under the protection of some saint. ... [A]s time went on, it solicited and paid for the titles of "noble" and "loyal" or others of similar nature, with the corresponding coat of arms; the streets [were] traced, at least in theory, with a rope; [there were] many convents, nunneries and churches; the rectangular plaza, when it was not near the landing of the harbour, [was] in the center of the city. . . . Our city had its symbol, its heart, in the plaza. It was the first thing to be traced when the city was founded and immediately the picota [the scaffold or tree of justice] was raised, as a sign that the new town would have gallows and knife, that is, civil and criminal jurisdiction in all its districts. Generally gathered around the plaza were the church, the casa de gobierno [house of the colonial authority], the cabildo [town hall] and the prison.[7]

The city was, as we have said, the first foothold of Spanish penetration in the unknown vastness of the new continent. In the beginning, the municipal corporations extended their jurisdiction over all the surrounding unpreempted lands and attributed them as property to the town-dwellers who claimed them. (The attribution of Indian workhands, as we know, was reserved to the highest royal authorities.)[8] To the first settlers and their descendants, the Crown granted, on the basis of their patrimony, the title of hijosdalgo de solar conocido (roughly "nobleman of well-known estate"). The principle underlying this title (that is, "the quality of conquistador or first settler, transmitted to the descendants, who form what the jurists of the XVIIth century call the 'well-deserving of the Indies'"), says Góngora, "consti-

---

[7]Op. cit., pp. 36-37.

[8]In Haring's words: "The town retained something of the character of the ancient civitas, or city state. It was more than an urban community; it included a large surrounding district as well, each town in the more settled regions extending to the bounds of its neighbors. In less settled areas, where towns were separated by stretches of wilderness, their jurisdiction might cover a widespread territory. The jurisdiction of Buenos Aires, for example, extended about 300 miles to the limits of that of Cordoba, about 170 miles toward Santa Fe, and southward as far as the Pampas Indians could be held in check. The territory of Popayan measured 66 miles to the neighborhood of Cali which bounded it on the north, and 60 miles to Almaguer on the south. The Spanish-American provinces, therefore, were in many instances a collection of municipalities, the latter, as someone said, being the bricks of which the whole political structure was compacted" (op. cit., p. 150).

PATTERNS OF URBANIZATION AND URBAN ATTITUDES

tutes the conscience of the ruling groups of each province, although their members did not always own encomiendas and often, in fact, did not actually descend from the conquistadors, since we deal here with the phenomenon of social consciousness rather than genealogy."[9]

There were other class rankings within the cities. There was the status of vecino, for example, which included all those who owned and inhabited a house in the town: the aristocracy of encomenderos, the rich merchants (in all comparable to the encomenderos), some men of arms, and the "lower classes" of small retailers and artisans. There was also the rank of hidalguía, which was less a factor of class, setting a social group based on common objective characteristics against another with different characteristics, than a principle of status used by the early plutocracies to establish a social distance between themselves and the less fortunate latecomers. Reflecting the traditional principles of social differentiation (that is, essentially, in the first phase, the right to claim privileges and benefactions from the Crown), the households in the cities were arranged, in decreasing order of social importance, around the vertex of the plaza. To complete the microcosmic representation of the colonial world, at the outskirts of the town were the Indian, and later the Negro, burden-bearers, perhaps separated by a river, as in Lima, where, in the words of Basadre,

> the suburb of el Cercado arose across the river: there lived with their own ministers, more than a thousand Indian families, destined for work in the haciendas of the valleys, and trained in the doctrine by the fathers of the Company. Throughout the other suburbs, rustic homes sheltered the greater number of Negroes employed in the service of the city, for, as Montalvo says, "the Spaniards, as soon as they leave their homeland, adjust themselves to serve only with the greatest difficulty."[10]

The towns being the centers of the aristocracies and also representing, in Morse's words, "the intrusion of formal, metropolitan bureaucracy into an empty continent,"[11] it is not surprising that the conflicts between the patrimonial king and his vassals arose and were quelled in the urban nuclei. The moves toward autonomy and the angry claims of the encomendero groups found their embodiment in the powerful and outspoken cabildos of the

---

[9] Op. cit., p. 186.

[10] Op. cit., p. 74.

[11] "Latin American Urban History."

first phase of colonization. However, when royal control was asserted, the cabildos were reduced to the almost total subordination that was their fate until 1810, the spontaneity and independence of the towns were definitively curtailed, and "their organization and activities regulated in minutest detail by laws framed in the council chambers of the king."[12]

The urban settlements of the New World had, since the beginning, a provisional character. The frequent urban transfers reflected, says Morse, "the unstable equilibrium of a continent not internally knit by exchange and commerce." After the first phase of vigorous communal autonomy, the pathologic signs were accentuated:

> The city was an outpost of metropolitan bureaucracy, imperial and ecclesiastic, in which status and function were determined by royal appointment. On lands surrounding the city, and in smaller towns, they were controlled by persons who soon preempted the soil and Indian labor. Those who were not favored by privilege or bound to the land in servitude, faced the choice of living parasitically off the vested interests or of scattering from the centers of settlement centrifugally in search of windfalls and unpreempted productive lands.[13]

The features of the urban phenomenon that we have thus far considered all converge toward the same conclusion. The towns of Spanish America, obviously enough, did not arise, as they did in medieval Europe, in an intimate, albeit contradictory, connection with their environment. Nor was their growth essentially determined by the emergence, from within the society, of certain strata "who could appropriate for themselves part of the produce grown by the cultivators" and hence live in towns, "because their power over goods did not depend on their presence on the land as such."[14] Their existence did not depend on the development of new economic functions and new forms of specialization, nor did their expansion disclose revolutionary potentialities conflicting with the preexisting social system. From the start, the Spanish American towns were a paramount characteristic of conquest, the implantation over the conquered territory of a preexistent and alien model of social organization. From the beginning, this

---

[12]Haring, op. cit., p. 149.

[13]"Latin American Urban History," p. 33.

[14]K. Davis, "The Origin and Growth of Urbanization in the World," American Journal of Sociology, LX, 5, March, 1955, pp. 429-37.

PATTERNS OF URBANIZATION AND URBAN ATTITUDES

pattern of colonization presupposed the appropriation of rural surpluses by a group of urban-based conquerors and settlers. Dispersion of the subjects resulted in encroachments on the sphere of patrimonial power; on the other hand, their concentration in towns aided in their subordination to the royal administrative apparatus. In this sense, the Spanish American towns were, essentially, the knots, the visible nuclei of the absolutistic patrimonial network. One point, relevant for later analysis, should be made here: Far from representing an "original" autonomous pattern with "revolutionary" potentialities, urban life represented one of the strongest links of the Creole elites with the patrimonial power. However, the towns related differently to the organizing principles of the Spanish order.

THE URBAN PHENOMENON AS AN EXPRESSION OF THE MERCANTILIST SYSTEM

Despite the instability and the centrifugal trends stressed by Morse, many towns of Spanish America survived and eveloped. We shall suggest here that the differentiation of the towns can be based on two sets of relationships. As Alessandro Pizzorno has written in his discussion of economic development and urbanization, the organization of cities involves two fundamental elements--"the relationship between the city and the rest of the territory, and the relationship between the city and the rest of the system."[15]

The larger system to which the Spanish American towns related was obviously the political and social structure whose patrimonial characteristics we have heretofore defined. On the other hand, given the mercantilist economic structure, the main determinant of the type of relations between town and territory was the existence (or the lack) of a marketable production. On these bases, it should be possible to categorize the differences between towns in the form of a very simple typology.

		TYPE OF MARKET TO WHICH PRODUCTION IS DESTINED	
		+ International (metropolitan Spain)	- Local
RELATIONSHIPS WITH THE BUREAUCRATIC- PATRIMONIAL ORDER	+	Bureaucratic and commercial capitals	Frontier towns and military garrisons
	-	"Relay" towns (mining towns in particular)	Isolated, "self-contained" units

---

[15]"Sviluppo economico e urbanizzazione," *Quaderni di sociologia* (Torino), XI, 1, 1962. [My translation.]

SPANISH BUREAUCRATIC-PATRIMONIALISM IN AMERICA

This form is adopted here for purposes of clarity only, but it is obviously inadequate to deal with the changing position of the towns. Changes took place, in particular, along the axis of relations with the market: these depended on the penetration of the hinterland and on the demand for the staples produced. Thus, as Celso Furtado and Aldo Ferrer, among others, have pointed out, the cycles of development--(1) "boom," (2) closure of the international market (or exhaustion of the source of production, as in the case of mining, in particular), and (3) depression (extended to the area which depended upon and thrived in the wake of the "boom" town)--are frequent in the history of Spanish American economies (as well as in the more recent history of societies subordinate to economic imperialism). When an important commercial circuit closes, an apparently prosperous economy may enter a phase of decay and its urban center revert to an almost subsistence economy characterized by the chronic lack of liquid capital. It is no longer possible to place the production on the international (or inter-regional) markets; consequently, the possibilities of buying manufactured or consumption goods (or, in general, goods that are not produced locally) decline sharply. Accordingly, the towns of decaying economic systems (namely, the "relay" towns) tend to become "isolated, 'self-contained' units." In these towns the "centrifugal" tendencies cannot be overcome.

A town's "relationship with the 'patrimonial order'" is easier to define. Since it is based mainly on the linkage with the bureaucratic-patrimonial structure, a possible index is the rank of the Spanish officials resident in the town--towns with a resident viceroy, captain-general, or _audiencia_ (+), towns where only a governor, _corregidor,_ or lesser official resides (-).[16] The frontier towns and military garrisons are special cases. Their position at the frontier of the empire requires, in our opinion, a strong relationship with the bureaucratic structure: whatever the effective control may be, the boundaries of a system are, in theory, as important as the center for its definition. However, the inclusion of towns in these categories is often only temporary, since the market position of such towns will depend on the penetration of the territory achieved. (The penetration determines the kind of production it will place on the market.)

An example of a bureaucratic and commercial capital was Lima--"residence of the viceroy, of his employees and dependents; of the _audiencia,_ with its _oidores,_ lawyers, prosecutors, and notaries; of the archbishop, of the metropolitan _cabildo_ and its

---

[16] The crossing of a discrete ordering with a continuum poses methodological problems which should be seriously considered. However, the diagram is presented here only to clarify the discussion.

PATTERNS OF URBANIZATION AND URBAN ATTITUDES

following; of the university, with its doctors and students; of the nobler and wealthier families."[17] Besides being the capital of the most extensive viceroyalty of the empire, Lima was close to the sea. Its harbor of El Callao made it a center of international exchange and distribution. Most of the administrative and economic activities of the Spanish colonies of South America converged for a long time in Lima. In 1770, it had 57,500 inhabitants, compared to the 22,000 of Buenos Aires. (This was six years prior to the latter's becoming the capital of the new viceroyalty of the Rio de la Plata.) The urban development of the bureaucratic centers such as Buenos Aires and Santiago, struggling to assert themselves commercially against the monopoly of Peruvian merchants, provides an interesting comparison with the urban development of Lima, where both political and economic primacy converged.[18] As the provincial capital of a presidencia (Chile was not elevated until 1778 to the rank of captaincy-general), Santiago de Chile had, by 1810, 30,000 inhabitants. Its "centrifugal" tendencies seem to have affected the rest of the presidency: the king had to order "that the Spaniards be confined to cities and towns to avoid their dispersion in ranchos, haciendas, and chacras."[19]

No other city in Chile, at the time, had more than 6,000 inhabitants. Notwithstanding its local predominance, Santiago appears to have been quite isolated both from the "center" of the empire and the rest of the continent. It was united to Concepción, the principal town of the south, by only two posts a month. A semiweekly service linked it to its port, Valparaíso, from where most of the exports were directed to Peru. Its main connections with Spain itself came by way of Buenos Aires. At the end of the eighteenth century a ship left La Coruña, Spain, every two months carrying mail for the Rio de la Plata, Chile, and the southern part of the viceroyalty of Peru, as far as Lima. It took two months, approximately, to reach Montevideo or Buenos Aires, and from there still another month was needed to get to Santiago by land. One consequence of this isolation and of the economic subordination to Peru was a rising volume of contraband trade with France and the United States.[20]

---

[17]Basadre, op. cit., p. 74. [My translation.]

[18]See Morse, "Latin American Urban History," pp. 324-25, and also Guillermo Céspedes del Castillo, Lima y Buenos Aires, repercusiones económicas y políticas de la creación del Virreinato del Río de la Plata (Seville, 1947).

[19]Quoted in Basadre, op. cit.

[20]See Hernán Ramírez Necochea, Antecedentes económicos de la independencia de Chile (Santiago: Prensas de la Editorial Universitaria, 1951).

SPANISH BUREAUCRATIC-PATRIMONIALISM IN AMERICA

The second type of city--the "relay" town--included the towns placed along the main axes of inter-regional traffic, or created at the confluence of various lines of communication. An example of the latter is Arequipa, "born to be a center between the Cuzco, the sea, and the minerals of Charcas."[21] As we have mentioned before, the northwestern Argentine towns placed on the routes to Alto Perú, such as Tucumán, or at the point of convergence of the road from Buenos Aires to Chile and the road to the mining regions of the North, such as Mendoza, owed their prosperity to their advantageous geographic positions. The traffic of cattle between the Rio de la Plata and the North or the Pacific coast was, for these towns, one of the main factors of development:

> Mules, horses, sheep, and cows were raised in the plains of Buenos Aires, Santa Fe, Corrientes, and Córdoba; they hibernated in Córdoba or Tucumán and, from there, passed to the periodic fairs of Jujuy and Salta. The herds left thence for different destinations: some toward Chile, some others towards the Alto and Bajo Perú. . . . The fair of the Lerma valley was, at the time [seventeenth century], one of the greatest of the world, with more than 60,000 mules and 4,000 horses, sheep, and cows distributed in its corrals; several thousand persons came from various parts of South America to participate, in one or another condition, to that continental market which was held every year during more than a month.[22]

Buenos Aires' commercial awakening had been slowed until 1778 by the repeated need to obtain special privileges from the Crown for commercial activities. The rules of free trade issued in 1778--two years after Buenos Aires had been elevated to the rank of viceroyalty capital--greatly improved the commercial position of both Buenos Aires and Montevideo. However, since the coastal regions did not produce at any time any major exportable goods for the European markets, the most important consequence was the right to receive imported goods and ship them to the towns of the interior, activities previously barred by internal custom duties. (The custom barrier established at Córdoba in 1622 had already been transferred earlier in the eighteenth century to Salta and Jujuy in the North.) As a result, the hinterland was rapidly "captured" by the European imports that were now more accessible than before the opening of the Rio de la Plata. However, the development of the provincial economies still depended above all on their limited inter-regional markets. When the wars of independence--and, concomitantly, the decline in production of

---

[21]Basadre, op. cit.

[22]Sergio Bagú, Estructura social de la colonia (Buenos Aires: Ateneo, 1952), p. 88. [My translation.]

PATTERNS OF URBANIZATION AND URBAN ATTITUDES

the mines of Potosí--closed the commercial circuits of Alto Perú, the northwestern Argentine towns, defenseless against the European imports, regressed toward a relatively closed type of economy, that is, toward what we have named "isolated, 'self-contained' units."

The inter-regional centers of the "relay" type were either dependent on traffic routes originating elsewhere, or they were themselves at one end of the route linking one--or several--main production centers to their outlets. Such was the case of the monoproductive centers, and especially of the mining towns. The production of a staple in great demand in European markets gave to the latter their character of "boom cities," but oscillations of the market or the exhaustion of natural resources led to the "chain" decline of the greatest part of the regional trade and accessory industries.

The frontier towns and military garrisons had a somewhat provisional status. They were, in effect, the outposts of the empire. Such towns had their raison d'être in the expansion of the system. In other words, they were key points in the process of "irradiation from the center." If founded by metropolitan decision--such as the military garrisons on the frontier delimited by Indian incursions--they pertained, theoretically, to the "positive" side of the relations with Spain. Even then, however, they were isolated, and in practice could show a large degree of autonomy and independence. In our opinion, the settlements "spontaneously" founded by enterprising colonists (as well as the very special case of the settlements of the Brazilian bandeira) represent a marginal case. We can suppose that, in the beginning, they resembled the communities in our last category--that is, the "isolated, 'self-contained' units." Then, according to the type of relationships they established with the surrounding territory and with the Spanish bureaucratic authorities, they became one or another of the main types distinguished, or, in extreme cases, were abandoned.

The isolated units, it has been suggested, were characteristic of those regions where agriculture could not adapt to the demands of colonial trade nor find a sizeable local market for its produce. Accordingly, "small-scale agricultural production emerged as the basic economic unit."[23] In a hardly distinguishable town-territory relationship, presumably with a strong "centrifugal" movement of the landowners toward the scattered haciendas, these towns had the primary function of consuming the surplus

---

[23]Aldo Ferrer, Las Etapas de la economía argentina (Mexico y Buenos Aires: FCE, 1963), Chap. 1: "Las Economías regionales de subsistencia en el actual territorio argentino." [My translation.]

SPANISH BUREAUCRATIC-PATRIMONIALISM IN AMERICA

they extracted from their rural dependencies. The relationship being almost static, the generative functions of the town with regard to the surrounding territory tended to be nil. As urban nuclei, we can suppose that these "rural" towns were limited to being the center of some collective activities. We know, for instance, that in "the little towns of XVIIIth century Puerto Rico . . . on Sundays and feast days, the people rode into town on horseback, made themselves comfortable in their houses--or in other houses, as doors were not locked--then heard Mass and returned directly to the country."[24] Aldo Ferrer provides us with an illuminating economic description of these agglomerations in his discussion of the "subsistence economies" of Argentina at the end of the eighteenth century. He describes the old "relay" towns, threatened by the rise of the harbor of Buenos Aires and already reverting to almost subsistence level.

> The encomenderos, the landowners, the rudimentary merchant groups were the only ones who disposed of an income above the level of subsistence. . . . The monetary economy only penetrated the transactions destined for the commerce external to the region itself. . . . [Accordingly] the accumulation of capital was almost null and concentrated in the activities of exportation. . . . The self-sufficiency and diversification of the structure of production was based on the incapacity of the regional economies to integrate themselves [directly, we would add] to the colonial market. . . . From the sixteenth to the eighteenth centuries, self-sufficience was not the characteristic of development, but the sign of stagnation.[25]

PATTERNS OF URBAN LIFE

This analysis of the urban phenomenon has characterized the Spanish American town as the main inroad of the patrimonial structure of power into the New World context. We have tried to account for the regional diversity of the colonial empire, where the internal linkages were weakened by isolation and instability, and we have used the economic functions developed by originally "political" towns to categorize their actual relations with the "ideal" patrimonial model. Our next step will be to attempt to link the above distinctions with the various patterns of urban life. In order to give an idea of the position of the Creole elites within these towns, we shall try to sketch the patterns of

---

[24]Morse, "Latin American Urban History," p. 330.

[25]Op. cit., Chap. I.

PATTERNS OF URBANIZATION AND URBAN ATTITUDES

political behavior that developed, and the predominant patterns of consumption. The latter will be considered as an indicator of the eventual emergence of an "original" ethic and way of life. (An at least partial insight into the outlook of the leading group is essential to the understanding of the independence movements.) In our approach, we shall follow some suggestions made by Alessandro Pizzorno in his article on "accumulation, leisure and class relationships." He writes:

> [A group which] does not have to go through the lengthy initiation of social stifling and, hence, of conflict with the class of nobles, does not need to develop a rigorous and ascetic ethic which would provide a basis of contempt for the models of conspicuous consumption of the superior class.

Referring to the European bourgeoisie, he adds:

> Where the barriers [between the nobility and the rising bourgeoisie] were more rigid and the consumption models were not used for social competition, accumulation and success in work . . . became moral values and norms of behavior, replacing the quest for prestige; the latter derives from a certain level of consumption, from certain possibilities of leisure, and from the social relations hence established. By posing an _ideological_ alternative to the whole existing social system, the bourgeois class set in motion the mechanisms of social transformation within the context of economic growth.[26]

Our discussion will be centered on the two "purest" types of Spanish American cities--that is, the bureaucratic and commercial capitals and the isolated units--since our main purpose is to discuss the relationships of the Creole elites with the patrimonial model. The _cabildos_ being the only political body in which the Creoles were represented, we shall approach political behavior by an appraisal of the _cabildos_' role. The municipal institutions of Spanish America did not appear or evolve autonomously. The _cabildo_, as we know, was transplanted from the Castilian municipal context and endowed, by the legislative action of the Council of the Indies, with "a uniformity in ground plan and in political organization" which, says Haring, "was not true of Spanish towns."[27] Gradually, the _cabildo_ became completely subordinate to the Crown and to the local oligarchies.

---

[26] "Accumulation, loisirs et rapports de classe," _Esprit_, June, 1959, pp. 1000-1016. See, in particular, pp. 1004-1006. [My translation.]

[27] _Op. cit_.

SPANISH BUREAUCRATIC-PATRIMONIALISM IN AMERICA

The _regidores_--whose number varied from four to fifteen in the most important cities--in principle were to be elected annually by the property owners of the town, and could not be reelected until one year had passed. The two _alcaldes_ were supposedly named by the _regidores_ on every first of January, and could not be reelected until after _two_ years. "In fact," says Haring,

> it can easily be established that in most of the important cities of America, the appointment of _regidores_ was from earliest times entirely in the king's hands or in those of his colonial representatives, and that any privilege of election that may be granted to the _cabildo_ was a concession from the Crown.

Furthermore, in 1591,

> a _cedula_ ordered the viceroy of Perú "on account of the necessities of the Crown" to sell all vacant life _regimientos_ in the cities and towns where such existed and to add as many as seemed suitable, to be disposed of "at the prices which are usually paid and which seem just."

And in places where the _regimientos_ were annual, and people were ready to buy them for life, the annual posts were to be abolished and life offices to be sold

> "in the number which seem suitable according to the quality of these _pueblos_ and the number of _vecinos_." . . . At first appointments were for one life only but . . . in 1606 all vendable offices were granted in perpetuity, with a right of resale or bequest within the holder's lifetime on condition of paying, the first time a half, and thereafter a third part of their value into the royal exchequer.

Some offices, like that of _alcalde ordinario_, remained elective, but subject to confirmation by the viceroy or president or their proxies. The Spanish officials such as the exchequer officers, moreover, had right of vote in the _cabildo_, taking rank above the other _regidores_: "The governor or corregidor possessed the same right, if the town was his official residence; and in such cases he had the privilege of presiding at the sessions. Otherwise, his deputy, or the first or second alcalde, sat in the cabildo and presided over it."[28]

Little was to be expected, then, in terms of increased

---

[28]The preceding quotes are taken from Haring (_op. cit._, p. 150), whose discussion of the _cabildo_ (Chap. IX, pp. 151-65 in particular) we have closely followed.

political authority, by the holders of municipal offices. We tend to think, however, that more than the social prestige derived from an association with the royal hierarchy could be gained. Besides their judicial functions as first instance courts,

> the cabildos exercised the normal, routine functions of [a municipal corporation]; that is, they distributed land to the citizens, imposed local taxes, provded for local police, levied a militia for defense in time of danger, gave building permits, maintained jails and roads, inspected hospitals, regulated public holidays and processions, supervised local market prices for the protection of the consumer, etc. . . . [But] by law, the regidores and alcaldes might not engage in trade directly or indirectly without royal permission, be associated with municipal contracts, or hold any other city office; and in some places, it seems, they received no salary.[29]

What compliance could be expected with these rules in a system where offices were generally regarded as prebends and where the remote units were practically impossible to control? It is more than likely that, in large bureaucratic towns such as Lima, where the hierarchy was tightly knit, and the Crown was represented by a high official, the political possibilities opened by a position in the cabildo were normally rather meager. However, ceremonial life being important in the life of the bureaucratic capital, the municipal offices automatically conferred on their occupants a place in the dominant scale of social prestige. Furthermore, the municipal funds were relatively large, as was the volume of city affairs that came under the cabildo's jurisdiction; accordingly, the possibilities of graft, in a system of widespread corruption, must have contributed to make the municipal offices attractive. In addition, the cabildos had the privilege of direct communication with the king and were in direct contact with local authorities.

In emergencies or exceptional cases, the measures to be taken were discussed in ad hoc assemblies called cabildos abiertos; invitations to participate in the deliberations were extended to the bishop and the clergy as well as to the notable citizens of the community. Thus, in times of crisis, the cabildos--and especially the cabildos abiertos--became important channels of influence, if for no other reason than that they were the only legal way by which the opinion of a part of the Creole group could be expressed. Thus, in Santiago, in 1776, the citizens directly concerned by the tax reforms of the treasury demanded, and finally obtained, the holding of a cabildo abierto. The frequent inter-

---

[29]Ibid.

vention of the cabildos in most of the anti-taxation movements in the last years of the empire tends to show that, however underrepresented or uninterested they were in the municipal corporations, the Creole elites in major cities found in them nonetheless the sole institutional voicing of their claims.

In some towns, such as Buenos Aires, for instance, offices were sold by public auction in the plaza, but we know that they were not in great demand, because of their low price. Thus, "after various vicissitudes, the cabildo of Buenos Aires, in the middle of the XVIIIth century received from the king the privilege of annually electing six regidores and compelling them to serve."[30] If this was true of a viceregal capital (however "atypical" or isolated it may have been), it is a likely hypothesis that, in very small urban societies, the most influential Creoles had other means than the cabildos to bring pressure to bear when their interests were concerned. The representatives of the Crown in the "isolated units" were, presumably, corregidores or tenientes (subordinate to the former). As we know, they were the weak links in the structure of bureaucratic control. They were often of Creole origin, although born in other provinces. Their power, notwithstanding this, was very extensive:

> The local governor was at once the political leader of the province, its legislator in matters of local policy, generally the commander-in-chief of its military establishment if there was one, and its most important judicial officer. But his salary was small, sometimes a percentage of the local revenues, and he had every temptation to increase his income from extra-legal sources.[31]

The economic exploitation of the Indians was, in many cases, a most profitable method of obtaining additional income. Furthermore, it is reasonable to suppose that the minor Spanish officials worked in collusion with the local oligarchies in a manner similar to that described by Bourricaud in today's Peru. Referring to the relationships of the inland "gamonales" with the agents of the central government, he says:

> These great landowners, who exploit an unqualified labor force and place on the market some low-priced products, belong to the oligarchy, even if they are not one of its most characteristic elements. To obtain an exact measure of their power, we ought to distinguish the regional level from the national. . . . At the local level, the "gamonal" is still

---

[30] Ibid.

[31] Ibid., p. 133.

the "boss" and disposes of an influence grounded on the delicate mechanisms of "caciquismo."[32]

Is it too hazardous to suppose that, in the remote and isolated towns of the Spanish empire, the interests of the imperfectly bureaucratized corregidores could be brought to coincide with those of the Creole "rural" elites? In this case, the lack of political participation of the latter would have quite a different meaning than merely apathy in response to subordination and exclusion. In a situation of de facto alliance, the need of access to the formal political structure is less pressing than in a "pure" case of political discrimination. But the local situation changed when such "modern" bureaucrats as the intendentes and their subdelegates replaced the easily corruptible corregidores and local governors.

Prior to 1803, the year in which the Nueva Ordenanza was published, the provincial cabildos were on the whole immersed in the lethargy of routine and prestige-seeking activities. After that, the intendentes arrived, whose action, especially in the Rio de la Plata, was to bring, in many cases, more changes, improvements, and dynamism than had ever been seen in the slumbering towns of the interior. Their reforms, however, meant a still greater degree of centralization, and the Creoles found themselves even more isolated than before, with fewer prospects of access--direct or indirect--to the colonial administration. Thus, the action of these generally progressive and energetic new administrators had a direct bearing on the awakening of the pre-Independence cabildos (and presumably on the interest the local elites took in them). John Lynch describes the awakening process in the Rio de la Plata in particular:

> The intendants certainly took the initiative in administration. But this did not mean that they took the initiative from the cabildos, for they could not take what the cabildos did not have. In fact, indirectly, the intendants aroused the cabildos of the viceroyalty of the Rio de la Plata from their lethargy. By increasing their revenue and by giving them more work to do, the intendants provided the cabildos with a new view of municipal government and a new prospect of urban development. Encouraged by their association with the work of the intendants and by the respect with which the early intendants treated them, the cabildos warmed to their new masters and cooperated happily with them. Then, as they became more sure of themselves, they began to resent the

---

[32]François Bourricaud, "Remarques sur l'oligarchie péruvienne," Revue française de science politique, Vol. XIV, 4, August, 1964, pp. 680-81. [My translation.]

SPANISH BUREAUCRATIC-PATRIMONIALISM IN AMERICA

tutelage of the intendants: anxious to control the funds which the intendants had made possible and to direct the work which the intendants had initiated, they reacted against their masters and began to claim more share of local government. Such a claim was naturally rejected and thereupon began a conflict between cabildos and intendants which characterized local government in almost all parts of the viceroyalty in the last years of Spanish rule and which gave the cabildos yet further training in municipal responsibilities.[33]

To conclude this discussion of the political situation in the "isolated units," we will quote Romero's remarks on the remote provinces of the Rio de la Plata. He says:

The municipal regime was bound to conflict with the authoritarianism of the Crown which, in effect, as exercised by the conquerors and the royal officials, above all in Buenos Aires, invalidated its original juridical organization, depriving it of its normal attributes and eventually conferring on it others that in fact lay outside its true jurisdiction. But [the municipal regime] had to struggle even more with rural reality, which not only lay outside the framework of municipal government but, in consequence, remained practically outside the law, except for circumstantial and sporadic actions. . . . Nonetheless, the discretional use of power and the abuse of privilege were masked by a solemn acknowledgment of the monarch's absolute authority, which, when it was able to make itself felt, operated, in fact, with those same characteristics.[34]

In the smaller "rural" towns the central authority faced the disintegrative influence of the countryside. Its control of the surrounding territory was weak. It was not sustained by strong currents of trade nor by effective authority. Power was fragmented in the de facto jurisdiction gained by each hacendado on his estate, or reduced to the superiority of force and ability, coupled with chance, as in the vagrant pastoral life masterfully painted by Sarmiento in Facundo.[35] Nonetheless, the urban agglom-

---

[33] Spanish Colonial Administration 1782-1810: The Intendant System in the Viceroyalty of the Rio de la Plata (London: Athlone Press, University of London, 1958), p. 287.

[34] José Luis Romero, A History of Argentine Political Thought, trans. by Thomas McGann (Stanford University Press, 1963), pp. 30-31.

[35] D. F. Sarmiento, Facundo. Translated into English under the title of Life in the Argentine Republic in the Days of the Tyrants (New York: Collier Books, 1961).

PATTERNS OF URBANIZATION AND URBAN ATTITUDES

eration bore witness to the presence of royal authority. Amidst "centrifugal" forces, the town was an attempt to introduce the administrative organization of the empire.

We suggested that, in the phase of "municipal lethargy," the political influence of the landowners in the towns was exercised through informal pressures on the royal representatives. The collusion of interests that eventually resulted represented the adjustment of central authority (in the person of its most unreliable or uncontrollable representatives) to an ungovernable reality. On the eve of Independence, the cabildos, we are told, had regained some life. When royal power receded, they were the only political bodies that could attempt to nucleate authority in the community. In the words of Bernard Moses:

> The people of the cities had a voice in the construction of the municipal corporations [the cabildos], and for this reason they might continue to act even if the power of the king was set aside and all the royal officers withdrawn. In the beginning of the period of emancipation, they alone stood between the people and social chaos.[36]

The "people of the cities," however, represented a small coalition of Creole landowners and vecinos. What power the cabildos could muster represented thus the power and the interests of the local elites, which ruled unchallenged after the withdrawal of the king's authority. In the troubled post-Independence years, if the municipal corporations retained a substantial political role, it was as the spokesmen for fragmentary, regionalist, and--in extreme cases --separatist views. However, in most cases, the smaller towns of the interior witnessed the rise of one man, or one faction, who prevailed over the other de facto rulers. In this light, the "age of the caudillos" can be seen as the emergence of what Morse called the "recessive traits" of the absolutistic patrimonial rule--that is, the spread of "independent" patrimonial power (or the power of improvised condottieri) from the rural areas, where it was entrenched, into the towns, where local supremacy became profitable and significant.

This is to restate in somewhat different terms the conflict central to Sarmiento's analysis of Argentina. The rise of the caudillos was a part, for him, of the wider struggle of civilization against barbarism, of city against country, in the unsettled context of the New World. However, in his polemical work, he doesn't fail to see that the "barbarous" pastoral life of Argentina represented also, to a certain extent, the cultural "origi-

---

[36] South America on the Eve of Emancipation (New York/London: G. Putnam & Sons, 1908), p. 97.

nality" (or the cultural "resistance") of America. Thus, he writes

> It cannot be denied that this state of things, on the other hand, has its poetic side. . . . If any form of national literature shall appear in these American societies, it must result from the description of the mighty scenes of nature, and still more from the illustration of the struggle between European civilization and native barbarism, between mind and matter--a struggle of imposing magnitude in South America, and which suggests scenes so peculiar, so characteristic, and so far outside the circle of ideas in which the European mind has been educated, that their dramatic relations would be unrecognized machinery, except in the country in which they are found.[37]

In Sarmiento's view, a fierce, authoritarian individualism bred by telluric forces invaded the towns in the "days of the tyrants," submerging the only distinguishable sources of progress and civilization, namely, Spanish urban tradition and, in general, European influence. Leaving value judgments aside, it remains true that whatever specific, "original" ways of life may have developed in the New World stemmed from a rural, not from an urban, context. This is consistent with the heteronomous nature of the cities which we have stressed thus far, and with the limitations of royal bureaucracy. "Although the colonial system was thought of as a set of institutions aimed at creating an essentially urban order," says Romero, "the economic life of the colony was supported in great part by the countryside, which escaped inclusion in the more rigid state structure."[38] Apparently, for the Creole elites, this duality was embedded in their way of life. Writing of a city as sophisticated as Lima in the eighteenth century, Leguía says:

> Although they obeyed French fashions and led in the drawing-rooms the life of the courtier, our nobles did not shrink from the habits of the purest "criollismo." In given periods of the year, they were subjected in the city to the tyranny of etiquette . . .; however, there were periods in which they could indulge freely in their desire for spontaneity.[39]

These were the summer months, spent on their country estates, or in their orchards in the suburbs of el Cercado. Conversely, in the provinces, small urbanized elite groups modeled their life,

---

[37] Op. cit., pp. 39-40.

[38] Op. cit., p. 29.

[39] Jorge Guillermo Leguía, Lima en el siglo XVIII (Lima: Ed. Euforion, 1921), pp. 31-32. [My translation.]

PATTERNS OF URBANIZATION AND URBAN ATTITUDES

their leisure, and their style and patterns of consumption on the more brilliant towns to which they went as students, professionals, travelers, or, later, as congressmen or provincial representatives.

The call to independence came generally from the major cities of the empire (the three foci were Mexico, Santa Fe, and Buenos Aires, with the Spanish resistance centered in Lima), but it remains to be seen whether, in the bureaucratic and commercial capitals, Creole patterns of life led to the emergence of a new class, radically opposed to the preceding system in terms of a distinct world view and opposed sets of values, and capable of mobilizing and uniting under its command the traditional "rural" elites of the provinces. Historical sources present the Creole elites of the major cities as a subordinate group. For the most part, they were barred from administrative or political careers. Imbued with status pride and yet excluded from the most prestigious occupations, the young Creoles of prominent families, having completed their studies in Spain or in the colonial universities, sought the few activities open to them which could be practiced without a feeling of social debasement. The most frequent were commerce (in the shadow of the monopolistic peninsular merchants), the law (which made them auxiliaries of the colonial agencies), the Church, and the colonial universities. Thus, in 1639, Father Cobo remarked that all the professorships at the University of San Marcos in Lima were held by Creoles, most of whom were graduates of the same university. The attempts to pursue a civil or military career in Spain confronted them with a system which formally recognized them as Spaniards but, in reality, ignored their existence and aspirations.

Leisure--whether unavoidable or voluntary--was an important characteristic of the life of the Creole elites in the bureaucratic capitals. These elites remained tied to the land from which most of their revenues derived. While in the "rural" towns some <u>hacendados</u> could find a time-consuming occupation in the direction of their estates (although, given the primitive conditions of production, this must have been rather exceptional), the professions accessible to them in the major cities hardly represented fulltime occupations. Subordination--that is, lack of opportunities and of social recognition--and leisure bred in them the idleness and nonchalance which the Spaniards considered to be inherent characteristics of the Creole aristocrats. Arrogance and pride, on the other hand, were normal in a group which, considering itself "superior" to all the other colonial strata, was systematically downgraded by the representatives of the Spanish order. This ambiguous position was bound to create growing feelings of resentment and estrangement, as new contacts and influences made them increasingly aware of other possibilities and alternative ways of life.

At the end of the eighteenth century, Don Alonso de Guzman,

SPANISH BUREAUCRATIC-PATRIMONIALISM IN AMERICA

a professional lawyer in the colonial administration, summed up the situation in his native Chile in a letter to the king:

> In the vast lands of the Indies, Your Majesty owns the allegiance of innumerable young men of great loyalty and talent but stifled in their own country for lack of prospects; the dreary idleness to which they are condemned depreives them even of the consolation of travel, and their minds are empty of useful ideas. The status of the Creoles has thus become an enigma: they are neither foreigners nor nationals . . . and are honorable but hopeless, loyal but disinherited. . . . Those who come [to Madrid] with the intention of following a career have nobody to sponsor them and are forced to speak for themselves. Their applications are very unwelcome, especially if they are directed to some of the ministers. . . . Disappointments like these embitter the hearts of these men. They see that as long as they live in America they can only be priests and lawyers, while in Spain they are at the mercy of a system in which they have no appointed place.[40]

Notwithstanding their subordinate position, the Creole elites were rich. In the trade-oriented colonial economies, the value of an investment depended chiefly on commerce which, as we know, was officially monopolized by the Spaniards. The entrepreneurial activities which, to start with, yielded but little social prestige, were thus dependent on the opening of the trade system. In this context, purchases of land, titles, and offices were the main outlets of new wealth. In other words, the rise of the new social groups (documented, among others, by Basadre, in Peru, and Edwards, in Chile) was not structured around the emergence of a new mode of production but, rather, derived from the impoverishment of the traditional aristocracies. The "upstarts" strove to gain access to the higher rungs of Creole society. Thus, in Lima, says Basadre, there was, at the time of the ascension of the new social groups, "an accentuation of the purchase of titles and coats of arms."[41] Creole wealth, then, was mainly used to the end of social emulation, following in this the patterns of consumption set by the peninsular "rivals," all too visible in the small but sophisticated urban societies. Conspicuous consumption had, in fact, become very early a characteristic of colonial urban life. In Lima, we are told,

> in the festive days it was impossible to distinguish those

---

[40] Quoted in Sergio Villalobos R., "The Creole Desire for Office," in R. A. Humphreys and John Lynch, eds., The Origins of the Latin American Revolutions (New York: A. Knopf, 1965), p. 253.

[41] Op. cit., p. 101.

who were nobles from those who were not. Montalvo and Menendez say that even the mulattoes wore silk, and changed their clothing according to the season, and that even in households without a coat of arms, one could see jewels and vases of silver or gold.[42]

As early as 1559, says Cobo, there were four or five carriages, and after thirty years there were more than two hundred, ornate with gold and lined with silk. "Indeed," he writes, "if there was moderation in this profanity, avoiding superfluous expenses, the inhabitants of this Republic would live more peacefully, without the strain and anguish brought by the will to sustain more brilliancy and authority than what they enjoy or may have."[43] The same is said of Mexico City by François Chevalier: "In this relatively poor country, the unprovidence and wastefulness of the _encomenderos_, as well as that of the miners and high official heirs, amazed contemporaries. 'This country's children are so prodigal that they spend every cent they own,' the Mexico City administration remarked in 1637."[44]

In the remote and seemingly more equalitarian society of Buenos Aires, the local elites applied in no different manner the riches gained from commerce, legal or illegal. To quote from García:

At the end of the seventeenth century, a French traveller writes the following . . .: "The greatest number of the merchants in cattle are very rich, but of all the merchants, the more important are those who trade in European merchandises, the fortune of many of these is evaluated near two hundred or three hundred thousand crowns, that is, sixty-seven thousand sterling pounds. Accordingly, the merchant who only has fifteen to twenty thousand crowns is considered as a mere retailer. Of the latter, there are close to two hundred families in the town. . . ."

In the celebration of Ferdinand VI's coronation, "the company of _vecinos_ appeared, riding in very expensive saddles, with beautiful reins and covers embroidered in gold and silver in Europe, or manufactured in this city with ornaments of gold and silver, and all of them dressed in very rich clothes that each had had made

---

[42]Ibid., p. 75.

[43]Quoted in ibid., p. 76.

[44]"The Formation of the Jesuit Wealth," in Magnus Mörner, ed., The Expulsion of the Jesuits from Latin America (New York: A. Knopf, 1965), p. 96.

for the occasion. . . ." And at the end of the seventeenth century, Azcarate du Biscay marvelled at the decoration of the houses: "Those of the first class inhabitants are adorned with hangings, paintings, and other ornaments and good furniture, and all those who enjoy a regular situation eat in silverware and have many servants."[45]

In an urban society geared more toward consumption than toward production, changes at this "suprastructural" level became clearly significant. Reflecting at once an estrangement from Spain and a new insistence on Creole identity, the models of consumption became increasingly inspired by France and placed a new stress on "Creole spirit." The appearance of "Creole spirit," says Basadre,

> had a political content; a social content because of the *de facto* inequality; an economic content brought about by the monopolistic regime; a literary content reflected in the appearance of an epigrammatic and popular genre in front of the stiff official literature; and it also had a typical content in food and clothing.[46]

The growing resentment of the Creole aristocracy was at first expressed in the appearance of new ways of life. Of this, clandestine agitation and intellectual heterodoxy--restricted, as they were, to a very small, cultivated minority--were, in a certain sense, a part.[47] Even in the long "loyalist" Lima, the secret societies (in particular the Masonic lodges), the *café* conversations, and the lively and active meetings of the *Sociedades de Amantes del País* (developmentist societies that were formed in several towns of Spanish America) replaced, for the young Creoles, the brilliant parties, the *tertulias*, the rides in the *paseo*, in which each carriage-owner would rather have his vehicle damaged than give up "his" side of the street. Leguía has vividly described the mood of a typical young nobleman of the times:

> The French philosopher whose work he has been skimming has reminded him of the sad reality that surrounds him. He, a rich and noble Creole, born in the viceroyalty, is excluded from the various posts and privileges of government and ad-

---

[45]J. A. García, *La Ciudad indiana* (3a. ed.; Buenos Aires: Angel Estrada y Cia., n.d.), pp. 235-37. [My translation.]

[46]*Op. cit.*, pp. 135-36. See Basadre's description of the liberalization of mores in eighteenth century Lima, *ibid.*, pp. 100-101.

[47]García, *op. cit.*

PATTERNS OF URBANIZATION AND URBAN ATTITUDES

ministration, in favour of inept and miserable peninsulars. He, the owner of strong merchant houses, cannot trade freely with Europe; and although he pays high duties for transportation and sale, is obliged to buy, without any compensation whatsoever, the articles that come from Spain. He, who has heard from his teacher in San Carlos about the freedom of trade and thought in the Old World, wants a similar evolution for his country. The intolerant spirit of the kings of Madrid is not disposed to allow these reforms? Well, the example of the North American emancipation is latent. Other Creoles have the same ideas and the same purposes.[48]

However, the old viceregal capital was exempt until late of the open marks of discontent that accompanied the disintegration of Spanish bureaucratic-patrimonialism in America.

At the beginning of the nineteenth century, various processes and events had converged to produce an explosive climate of unrest which was perceptible throughout the empire.[49] We shall briefly recapitulate the most significant. The modernization of administration under the Bourbons had various effects. While it fostered economic development in the colonies and to a certain extent widened the possibilities of commercial and intellectual circulation, it did not entail political liberalization. According to Octavio Paz, New Spain (and the other American kingdoms) became then a colony in the true sense, that is, "a territory subject to systematic exploitation and strictly controlled by the center of power."[50] Under the new administration, the Creole elites found themselves as excluded as they ever had been from the higher charges; the officers appointed by Spain, moreover, sought to exercise a more effective, albeit more enlightened, control over the overseas territories.

The reality of the "causes" of Creole resentment has been questioned by Jaime Eyzaguirre. He argues that the main aspiration of the subordinate group was not to obtain access to the intermediate administrative offices, since "their predominance in the bureaucracy, at least from the middle of the eighteenth century, was unquestionable. . . . They aspired not merely to the majority of offices in their respective provinces but to all of them, to

---

[48] Op. cit., pp. 36-37.

[49] For a comprehensive discussion of this point, see Humphreys and Lynch, eds., op. cit.

[50] Quoted in R. Morse, "The Heritage of Latin America," in Louis Hartz, ed., The Founding of New Societies (New York: Harcourt, Brace & World, 1964), p. 166.

the total exclusion of the Spaniards."[51] Whatever the truth of this position as compared to those which argue that exclusion from office was one of the main causes of the independence movement, it remains true that the Creole elites became increasingly aware of their rights and impatient at the arbitrariness of the Crown.

The expulsion of the Jesuits by the king in 1767 further aggravated the situation. By the sale of Jesuit property, it is true, many Creole interests became vested in the permanence of the resulting redistribution. However, by and large, the expulsion meant economic involution for the regions where the Jesuits had practiced their particular form of capitalistic organization; in all of Spanish America, the best schools and universities were run by the fathers, and their departure meant a major intellectual loss. Many of the Jesuits, moreover, were American born: their exile was seen with great resentment by their families, friends, and disciples. The writings of some of the exiles, it has been said, contributed directly to the rise of Creole nationalism.[52]

Much has been said about the influence of French, English, and American liberalism on the upper-class minorities of the colonies. However, in the economic aspects as well as in others, Spanish liberalism and the enlightened despotism of the Bourbons were equally influential. Thus, the "regalist" policy practiced by the new dynasty with regard to the Church (with the systematic curtailment of church interference in state affairs that it involved) was an important sign of the weakening of the Hapsburgian "theocratic" state. Say Humphreys and Lynch:

> Despite the censorship of the Inquisition, the literature [of the Enlightenment] entered and circulated with comparative freedom . . . and the readers included higher civil servants, professional men and ecclesiastics, merchants, and even officials of the Inquisition itself. The flow seemed to have reached its height in the 1790's, and it was then that the Inquisition, hitherto half-hearted and inefficient, began to bestir itself, alarmed principally by the political and seditious content of some of the new writing, which was regarded as "contrary to the security of the states," imbued with "general principles of equality and liberty for all men,"

---

[51]"Promise and Prejudice in Spanish America," in Humphreys and Lynch, eds., *op. cit.*, p. 260.

[52]On these points, which we cannot discuss at length here, see Mörner, ed., *op. cit.*, and in Humphreys and Lynch, eds., *op. cit.*, see "Introduction" and articles by Ricardo Donoso ("Spanish America and the Expulsion of the Jesuits") and Miguel Batllori, S.J. ("The Role of the Jesuit Exiles").

and even spreading news of "the frightful revolution in France which caused such damage."[53]

---

[53]Op. cit., "Introduction," p. 12.
The different numbers of printing presses and/or periodicals in the various cities suggest different degrees of urban "sophistication" and, as well, differences in the size of the public reached by the new ideas. At the time of Vertiz's appointment to the post of second viceroy of the Rio de la Plata (1777), "the superiority of Buenos Aires," writes Bernard Moses, "lay solely in its geographic position." It had only "an old fort, a town organization and an old market." The viceroy gave to the town its first urban improvements, as well as its first press, brought from Córdoba where the Jesuits had left it. However, "he knew no one competent to set up the press and use it," and the first newspapers did not appear until 1801-1802. The Telégrafo Mercantil (1801-1802) was followed by the Semanario de Agricultura, directed by Hipólito Vieytes (1801-1807), then by the Correo de Comercio and the Gaceta de Buenos Aires, the newspaper of Bernardo Monteagudo, in 1810 [Moses, op. cit., p. 93 ff.]. According to Moses, the cabildo of Santiago de Chile had petitioned the king to establish a printing press in 1789, but without success. The first press arrived there in 1811, brought by a naturalized American citizen, together with three American typographers whose salary was equivalent to $1,000 a year [Moses, "Camilo Henríquez and La Aurora de Chile," in The Intellectual Background of the Revolution in Spanish-America (New York: Hispanic Society of America, 1926)]. Haring, op. cit., p. 230n., gives the following dates of appearance of presses in the eighteenth century: Havana, 1707 or 1724; Oaxaca, 1720; Bogotá, 1738-1742, 1777; Ambato, 1754; Quito, 1760; Valencia (Venezuela), 1764; Córdoba (Argentina), 1766-1767; Cartagena, 1769-1776; Santiago (Chile), 1776?; Buenos Aires, 1780; Santo Domingo, 1782?; Guadalajara, 1794; Veracruz, 1794; Santiago (Cuba), 1796. In Lima, on the other hand, the first press had been established in 1584: "Antonio Ricardo of Turin, who had been a printer in Mexico since 1577, three years later left for Lima, and in 1584 obtained royal permission and the sole right to establish a press there. But the press in Lima was never so active as that of Mexico, and typographically its productions were generally inferior." After Mexico and Guatemala, Lima produced a periodical in 1743, the Gaceta, which appeared until 1767. "To Lima also belongs the credit of producing the first daily newspaper in America, the Diario de Lima, curioso, erudito, económico y comercial, . . . which appeared for exactly three years, from October 1790 to September 1793. . . . [I]n January 1791 appeared the more celebrated Mercurio Peruano. Published by the Sociedad de amantes del país, which represented most of the intellectual and literary talent of the viceregal

SPANISH BUREAUCRATIC-PATRIMONIALISM IN AMERICA

To the latter event, particularly, the Creoles reacted. Although we are told that the names of Barere and Robespierre were known and quoted in popular conversations in the viceroyalty of the Rio de la Plata, "when the execution of the king became known, these sympathies cooled considerably, as happened in other countries."[54] In fact, for the most part, the Creole upper classes still nurtured feelings of overarching loyalty toward the Spanish monarch, as witnessed by the "legitimist" justifications of the first phase of the Independence wars. Organized sedition was unthinkable for most of them, although the interest in "seditious literature" was, in the words of a Chilean author, a source of consoling speculations and an intellectual pastime. As pointed out by Francisco Encina:

> Certain conditions were necessary before the ideology of the French revolution could have played its alleged role in the preparation of independence. The upper classes in Chile would have had to be sympathetic towards it, for these were the only ones at the time capable of accepting it. Or it would have had to be integrated into the Spanish tradition and adapted to its nature. Neither of these conditions existed. In the case of the Creole aristocracy, a mere declaration of the basic tenets of the Revolution would have been enough to send the majority of it to enlist in aid of the king.[55]

The opposition to the king's financial policy provides an illustration of both the extent of dissatisfaction and the partial character of the forerunning acts of protest. After the fiscal reforms of the Bourbons, anti-taxation movements, led by the Creole aristocracy and often voiced by the cabildos, spread in many cities. In Peru, in 1780, riots broke out in La Paz, Arequipa, Cochamba, Cuzco. In New Granada, in 1781, the more serious revolt

---

capital, it exerted a profound influence upon the cultural and political development of Peruvian society. Appearing every three days, half newspaper and half review, it yet was chiefly a literary, scientific and historical journal, including the ablest minds of the Creole community among its contributors, reflecting the intellectual curiosity of the time, the mouthpiece of a nascent Peruvian nationality. It survived till 1795" (Haring, op. cit., pp. 229-31).

[54] Ricardo R. Caillet-Bois, "The Rio de la Plata and the French Revolution," in Humphreys and Lynch, eds., op. cit., pp. 94-105.

[55] "The Limited Influence of the French Revolution," in Humphreys and Lynch, eds., op. cit., p. 109.

of the comuneros occurred. This revolt,

> like the unrest in other parts of the empire, had a specific cause--in this case the onerous tax measures of visitor-general Juan Francisco Gutierrez de Pineres, combined with what the Creole leaders regarded as "the intolerable harshness and crudeness of the tax collectors." . . . [The movement] had demonstrated that the Creoles were capable, on occasion, of communal action and were ready to protest against the abuse of power. Yet these protests were made within the existing regime: the comuneros demanded a change in administration and fiscal policy, not the end of imperial government.[56]

In Chile, as early as 1753, Concepción protested vehemently against a newly decreed monopoly of tobacco; "in Santiago the merchant body protested jointly with the Cabildo, requesting that the monopoly be limited to Perú."[57] Similar outbursts occurred in 1766 and in 1776, when the treasury accountant suppressed the farming out of the sales tax or alcabala, and set out to reform the tax on pulperías (authorized provision stores which paid an excise duty). The disturbances grew, and some pamphlets even went as far as openly attacking the policy of the Crown. The measures were finally rescinded, but it is extremely interesting to see some of the judgments made by contemporaries on the character of the agitation. Thus, a Creole writes to a friend in Spain:

> You may take it that there has been considerable unrest, but unrest that has not exceeded the limits of complaint against grievances, no more; and, therefore, the rumors of rebellion, insurrection, and aversion to the sovereign's policy . . . are irresponsible and unfounded, for I was an eye witness of all that happened, and I never observed among all the clamor any ideas unworthy of our country.

Manuel de Salas, the enlightened procurador of the audiencia, wrote: "[Had the regulations not been rescinded by decree] there would have been a rising in the country with fatal consequences. . . . You may be sure that the people of consequence, especially the cabildo, have suppressed the wild and insolent behavior of the huasos." And the president of the audiencia, on request of the Minister of the Indies, Gálvez, in his lengthy answer tried to explain the events and to diminish their threatening aspect:

---

[56] Humphreys and Lynch, eds., op. cit., "Introduction," pp. 16-18.

[57] This and the following quotations are taken from Sergio Villalobos R., "Opposition to Imperial Taxation," in Humphreys and Lynch, eds., op. cit., pp. 124-37.

SPANISH BUREAUCRATIC-PATRIMONIALISM IN AMERICA

It is my firm opinion and belief that the commotion and resistance among the people on this occasion was supported, or perhaps fostered, by a few private individuals of the highest rank. . . . It was not exceptional for the landed proprietors, among whom are counted the most substantial citizens of the city and the kingdom, and even for the judges then composing the royal <u>audiencia</u> . . . to regard the activities of the lower classes without concern and even with approval, as these were calculated to defend the <u>haciendas</u> from this alleged burden. . . . I am of the opinion that . . . both peace and loyalty are as respected, assured and deeply rooted in all the provinces of Chile as in any of the other provinces of the viceroyalty of Perú.

From the various elements presented, we can abstract the general attitude that prevailed among the urban Creole elites on the eve of Independence. Traditionally attached to the Crown, politically conservative, they mistrusted and feared the eventual stirring of the "subject races." Conscious of their uncertain status, they despised the lower classes of the cities, though eventually, as we shall see, they joined forces with them. Apparently, no group among the elites was powerful or determined enough to propose and sustain a comprehensive ideology of transformation that could have united the partial and disorganized expressions of discontent. However, the sources of dissatisfaction were general and increased in number and intensity with time. Although, in the words of Humphreys and Lynch, "it is all too easy to equate the forces of discontent or even the forces of change with the forces of revolution," unrest was sufficiently widespread to produce simultaneous outbreaks, in several points of the empire, of movements of protest.

V

THE REVOLUTIONARY CHALLENGE

At the beginning of the process of emancipation, the colonies responded to the seizure of Ferdinand VII of Spain by Napoleon, and to the following "nationalist, monarchist movement of resistance" in Spain, with a similarly "legitimist" answer. The establishment of provisional governments brought into the open the various trends toward reform. (Except for a very small minority of ideologues within the already small minority of activists, the first juntas were reformist, and not revolutionary in scope and attitude.) For Morse, the best analogue to the Spanish American wars for independence is the Protestant Reformation:

> Both movements occurred within a far-flung, venerable Catholic institutional order which was exhibiting decadence at its upper levels. Both movements developed as uncoordinated patterns of dispersed and disparate revolt. Neither was heralded by a coherent body of revolutionary doctrine, and each improvised its multiple "ideologies" under pressure of events. Indeed, each movement at its inception betrayed a strong conservative or fundamentalist character. Each was the final cluster of a centuries-old series of random and localized heresies, uprisings or seditions; and, in the case of each, world events were finally propitious to transform the impromptu outbreak into a world-historical revolution.[1]

The absence of a legitimate government in Spain created a situation which, according to the principles of the Suarezian doctrine, justified "a reversion of sovereignty to the people," as, in fact, was argued by Juan José Castelli in the <u>cabildo abierto</u> of May, 1810, in Buenos Aires.

The independence movement became separatist and Pan-American in character after the inept course taken in 1814 by the restored Ferdinand. What elements mainly contributed to the emergence of a "united front" of the Creole bourgeoisies in the peripheral foci (Mexico, Buenos Aires, Santa Fe) from which the movement toward continental independence radiated? We shall argue

---

[1] R. Morse, "The Heritage of Latin America," in Louis Hartz, ed., <u>The Founding of New Societies</u> (New York: Harcourt, Brace & World, 1964), p. 159.

that, in the cities which experienced a double subordination (with regard to Spain and with regard to the Spanish monopolistic merchants who resided locally or were based in Peru), social exclusion and, above all, economic motives, prevailed over political and ideological alignments.

Until 1819, economic grievance was the strongest cause of discontent and, in Romero's view, the factor that gave shape to the antagonism between peninsulars and Creoles, the latter supporting the tenets of physiocratic and liberal economic theories. In cities such as Buenos Aires and Santiago, the Creole elite had readily perceived and understood what could be gained from increased commercial contacts with the expansionist powers of the world. Free trade, free importation of European techniques, and the priority of local interests over imperial necessities were the conditions sine qua non for salvaging and developing the existing systems of production. This was clearly elaborated in Chile by José Cos Irriberi, Manuel de Salas, and Anselmo de la Cruz, in particular, and was perceptible in the enlightened policies of the great governor Ambrosio O'Higgins.[2] Similarly, in Buenos Aires, in 1809, Mariano Moreno, in his famous "Representación, en nombre de los labradores y hacendados de las campañas del Rio de la Plata" (Representation in the Name of the Farmers and Landowners of the Country of the Rio de la Plata), had coherently voiced the complaints that were among the primary concerns of the provisional juntas:

> Is it just that the abundant productions of the country should rot in our magazines, because the navy of Spain is too weak to export them? . . . Is it just that, when the subjects of a friendly and generous nation present themselves in our ports, and offer us, at a cheap rate, the merchandise of which we are in want, and with which Spain cannot supply us, we should reject their proposals and convert, by so doing, their good intentions to the exclusive advantage of a few European merchants who, by means of a contraband trade, render themselves masters of the whole imports of the country? Is it just that, when we are entreated to sell our accumulated agricultural produce we should, by refusing to do so, decree at the same time the ruin of our landed proprietors, of the country, and of society together?[3]

---

[2]Hernan Ramírez Necochea, Antecedentes económicos de la independencia de Chile (Santiago: Prensas de la Editorial Universitaria, 1951), esp. pp. 81-105.

[3]"Free Trade Versus Monopoly," reprinted in R. A. Humphreys and John Lynch, eds., The Origins of the Latin American Revolutions (New York: A. Knopf, 1965), pp. 187-88.

THE REVOLUTIONARY CHALLENGE

In other words, at the periphery of the empire, where economic claims were stronger and the targets of the movement more visible (the groups of privileged Spanish merchants being smaller, more cut off from the rest of the society, more vocal in formulating their reactions to the liberal measures of the juntas), the more "radical" groups of the Creole bourgeoisie achieved a de facto alliance with the urban masses. By so doing, they gained "popular" support for the secessionist movement and opened the way to its expansion.

In Lima, meanwhile, in the years from 1810 to 1818, "the nobility," writes Basadre,

> was still convinced of the importance that, in spite of everything, Lima and the viceroyalty had not lost; there were very many Spanish families, in particular in trade and in the bureaucracy; the capital enjoyed a situation of affluence. . . . Patriotic agitation was reduced, in Lima, to innovating teaching, to private meetings, to clandestine fancies, to the contact with the outside insurgents, to crazy conspiracies. . . . In these long years, denunciations, persecutions, isolated and uncautious plans, pitiless repressions predominated in Lima. It is then that the secret societies appear and become entrenched in Perú: official Masonic lodges, or lodges with a mere patriotic orientation.[4]

In the peripheral foci of the empire, various elements coalesced to form a driving move for independence that would finally overpower Peru, the bastion of Spanish resistance. Thus,

---

[4]Jorge Basadre, La Multitud, la ciudad y el campo en la historia del Perú (2a. ed.; Lima: Huascaran, 1947), pp. 142-43. [My trans.]

In 1822, Monteagudo, named minister of government and foreign affairs of Peru by San Martín, founded the Sociedad Patriótica de Lima. Among the subjects announced for prize essays or discussions by the members was "The Causes That Have Retarded the Revolution in Perú." A contemporary, José Morales, explains the lack of revolutionary leadership in Peru as follows: "[T]here was scarcely a Creole merchant in Lima; the majority were Europeans; and in order to maintain their ancient monopoly, they maintained a close and indissoluble league with the government. The nobles had their wealth in landed estates and other real property, the principal value of which consisted in the number of slaves who cultivated these lands; they were, therefore, naturally anxious to preserve the government which had created and approved of the system under which they had acquired their wealth." Quoted from Bernard Moses, The Intellectual Background of the Revolution in South America (New York: Hispanic Society of America, 1926), chapter on "Monteagudo as Minister of Perú."

SPANISH BUREAUCRATIC-PATRIMONIALISM IN AMERICA

in Colombia and the Rio de la Plata, the movement mustered "intellectual leadership for the revolution in the cities; popular uprisings in the country which at first were loyal to the king, but later joined the revolution; national military organization; American influences; and, lastly, constructive political thought."[5] To this was added the uncertain alliance of the "democratic" <u>caudillos</u> who had rallied the dispersed populations in the countryside and transformed them into "soldiers of the revolution." The presence of men such as José Artigas (Uruguay), José Güemes (Argentina), and José Paez (Venezuela), among others, at the side of the military leaders who came from the Creole urban militiae, foreordained the difficulties encountered at the end of the wars in creating legitimate central authorities in the new states. In spite of the "constructive political thought" of a group of leaders, the mobilization of the heterogeneous forces was not accompanied by even a minimum agreement on basic political ends.

Bolivar offered this analysis in his Jamaica letter:

> The Americans have risen rapidly without previous knowledge and, what is worse, without previous experience of the conduct of public affairs, to enact upon the world stage the important role of legislators, magistrates, financial administrators, diplomats, generals, and every position of authority, supreme or subordinate, that comprises the hierarchy of a fully established state.

And, arguing in Voltairian manner in favor of a government that would be suited to the reality of the new society, he adds:

> Events in Tierra Firme have proved that wholly representative institutions are not suited to our character, customs and present knowledge. . . . Thus, Venezuela, the American republic with the most advanced political institutions, has also been the clearest example of the unsuitability of the democratic and federal system for our newborn states. In New Granada, the excessive powers of the provincial governments and the lack of centralization of the federal government have reduced that fair country to its present condition. . . . As long as our countrymen do not acquire the political talents and virtues which distinguish our brothers of the north, wholly popular systems, far from working to our advantage will, I greatly fear, come to be our ruin.[6]

---

[5] Victor Andrés Belaúnde, "The Origins of Spanish-American Nationalism," in Humphreys and Lynch, eds., op. cit., p. 291.

[6] "Contestación de un americano meridional a un caballero de esta isla," translated and reprinted under the title "A Creole's Resentment," in Humphreys and Lynch, eds., op. cit., pp. 264-65.

THE REVOLUTIONARY CHALLENGE

For the statesmen of the time, almost without exception, "popular" government meant a parliamentary government modeled primarily on the English system, and elected by the literate male property owners. The fragmentation and disunity perceived by Bolivar reflected, then, the contradictory and vague orientations of the Creole bourgeoisies. As we have tried to show, the latter appeared more as a subordinate group than as a cohesive class structured by an autonomous economic drive and capable of rallying the dissenting factions around a "total" world view pitted against the "old order." "The independence of Spanish America," says Morse, "caused the decapitation of a realm that had ever been, if not unified, at least unitary." After the paternalistic and bureaucratic rule of the patrimonial monarch was withdrawn,

> it was impossible to identify a substitute authority that would command general assent. Decapitated, the government could not function, for the patrimonial regime had developed neither: (1) the underpinning of contractual vassalic relationships that capacitate the component parts of a feudal regime for autonomous life; nor, (2) a rationalized legal order not dependent for its operation and claims to assent upon personalistic intervention by the highest authority.[7]

Thus, the relative unity achieved in the heat of the struggle gave way to anarchy, except where a common denominator could be found that, replacing the opposition to the "Spanish oppressor," would unite the disparate Creole oligarchies at a "national" level. Where the danger or the reality of popular uprisings was present, counterrevolution could serve this function, especially after the liberal reforms of 1820 in Spain suggested, for chapetones and Creole oligarchs alike, a possible leniency of the mother country with regard to the colored underprivileged groups.

Where this alternative was too remote, the stability of the new governments seemed to depend on the emergence of a leader (or a faction) powerful and skilled enough to muster support for his own definition of legitimate authority. Since the compartmented patrimonial state had failed to create a group sufficiently cohesive to propose and affirm truly nationalist principles, power had to be generated, at the national level, either through the use of force (which meant, after the independence wars, a certain degree of control over the armed forces) or through the achievement of a de facto coalition among the significant factions of the Creole upper classes. In either case, given the limited number of participants in the political "game," the emerging national government would represent a form of oligarchic rule. The latter type of government could be qualified according to its degree of

---

[7]Morse, "The Heritage . . .," p. 161.

dependence upon the military.

Independence meant the insertion of the ex-Spanish American territories into a wider system of trade than they had known under Spanish rule. They remained economically subordinate, however, but now to expansionist foreign powers, not to a decaying one, as Spain had been. Therefore, we shall argue that the appearance of an oligarchy which could unify the new societies under its control required a condition that was attained sooner or later in the various states: the most "dynamic" groups in the hitherto stifled economies--that is, the commercial bourgeoisies of the coastal capitals or the propertied producers oriented toward international trade--had to prevail over the "centrifugal" forces which thus far had been relatively checked by the patrimonial bureaucracy. Accordingly, we propose to distinguish three distinct processes or spheres of historical action which, together, provide a comprehensive approach to the transitional period extending from the collapse of the Spanish order and the "traditional" sources of legitimacy to the consolidation of oligarchic rule.

The first is, traditionally, the subject matter of economic history. It involved the incorporation of the new states into wider circuits of trade. According to Aldo Ferrer, the integration into the national economies of the chief dynamic principle of the time--namely, international trade--determined a series of adjustments and readjustments which account for some fundamental processes undergone during the nineteenth and the first part of the twentieth centuries by Argentina and the other Spanish American states. This most fundamental, albeit partial, sphere of action includes important aspects of the transitional period: the struggle between the partisans of protectionist and laissez-faire policies (which underlies, for Miron Burgin, the conflict between centralism and federalism in Argentina),[8] the rise--or the decline--of the groups controlling the production, transportation, and export of the principal marketable products,[9] and the final prevalence of a coalition of exporters-producers depending on the heteronomous operation of international markets and on the local management of foreign capital.

Since local laissez-faire proponents faithfully followed

---

[8] The Economic Aspects of Argentine Federalism (Cambridge: Harvard University Press, 1946).

[9] Tulio Halperin Donghi, "La Expansión ganadera en la campaña de Buenos Aires," in Desarrollo Económico, III, 1-2, April-September, 1963, pp. 57-110. See also James Scobie, Argentina (New York: Oxford University Press, 1964), in particular Chap. 5, "An Agricultural Revolution in the Pampas."

THE REVOLUTIONARY CHALLENGE

the economic doctrines of the "modern" industrial powers of the world, the partisans of free trade often appeared to be strong advocates of "modernization." In relation to the economic processes, therefore, we find groups and policies which expressed a more or less superficial attempt to "modernize" the anachronistic structures inherited from the Spanish system of production and trade. However, in the abstract, free trade did not represent a discontinuity with respect to the colonial economic system. Although the national product was greatly diversified and expanded (resulting in a corresponding and, for us, more interesting modification and diversification of the social structure), and although the Creole bourgeoisies now contended among themselves for a share in the internal control of the commercial system, the dynamic parts of the economies of the new states were still "other-directed"--still dependent upon foreign markets and sources of capital uncontrolled and uncontrollable by local groups.

The second sphere of action is that of power politics. In this instance, it involved primarily the drive for power of the rurally-based <u>caudillos</u>, a "recessive" movement which, in Romero's words, represented the "line of inorganic, direct democracy."[10] (Morse, analyzing the <u>caudillo</u>, has remarked his resemblance to the Machiavellian prince.)[11] This drive for power involved armed bands organized under the "democratic" rule of a fortunate <u>caudillo</u> (whose autocratic power was founded on a "direct" contact with the marginal populations that he organized, by virtue of his charismatic influence) or the more paternalistic rule of a local patrimonial lord. According to the degree of success of their personalistic policies, the <u>caudillos</u> came to represent more or less wide regional and partisan interests. François Chevalier has argued that, in the sphere of "Machiavellian politics," the difference between the power of the local <u>caciques</u> and that of the national <u>caudillos</u> was not a difference in nature, but a difference of station.[12] The "invasions" of the cities by the countryside (studied by Sarmiento in <u>Facundo</u>) represents, in this view, the periods in which the organizing principles of economic interest and political centralization were partially ignored in what has been considered a naked "game" of power.

---

[10] José Luis Romero, <u>A History of Argentine Political Thought</u>, trans. by Thomas McGann (Stanford University Press, 1963).

[11] Morse, "Toward a Theory of Spanish American Government," reprinted from <u>The Journal of the History of Ideas</u>, XV, 1954, under the title "Political Theory and the Caudillo" in Hugh H. Hamill, ed., <u>Dictatorship in Spanish America</u> (New York: A. Knopf, 1965).

[12] François Chevalier, "The Roots of Personalismo," reprinted in Hamill, ed., <u>op. cit</u>.

SPANISH BUREAUCRATIC-PATRIMONIALISM IN AMERICA

The third process or sphere encompasses the attempts to organize the new states on a centralized national basis. The revolutions of independence did not--and could not--achieve a structural transformation of the societies issuing from the patrimonial order. Moreover, the programmatic liberalism of the small groups of ideologues failed to recognize and to adjust to the social and political realities of those countries where they had gained a temporary leadership. Their failure to muster sufficient support among the conservative forces, often alienated by premature or too drastic measures; their inferiority in the field of "Machiavellian politics" and, accordingly, an excessive dependence on the support of the armies; and, finally, the uncertain and slow course of the integration into the economic orbit of the expansionist industrial powers--all these combined to make the first phase of the rule of the liberal doctrinaires particularly vulnerable. Thus, the attempts to bring together the compartmented and disparate fragments of the patrimonial configuration, by submitting them to a new order which would reflect the supremacy of the enlightened and culturally "heteronomous" bourgeoisies of the primate cities, were generally unsuccessful. Since we are dealing with subordinate economies, in which the main stimuli for development came from external sources, any resemblances to the actions of the European national bourgeoisies were more in form than in substance. The "modernizing" values and actions of the Creole liberals were <u>inspired</u> by foreign models rather than determined by similar structural and historical conditions. The "modern" patterns and courses of action were mediated through the persistent structures and patterns of behavior derived from the centuries-old patrimonial bureaucratic order. At all levels of society, synthetic and transitional forms appeared which incorporated the "modernizing" influences into a specific historical matrix: from this crucible, we could say, autonomous and autochthonous orientations were subsequently derived.

The three processes distinguished could be said to define, in each national context, a series of partially overlapping "games" --comparable to circles, structured each by its own rules. At their intersection we would find the significant actions and processes that "bridged the gap" between the different spheres of action and defined the changing loci of "national" politics. Coalitions and compromises, alliances between <u>caudillos</u> and prevailing economic interests, sheer acts of power, interplay of regional interests, attempts to enforce financial and economic policies of wide scope--all of these helped to prepare for the emergence of the "unifying factor." The resulting dominant force was --in different concrete forms--the more or less stable and homogeneous oligarchic coalition which, for so long, imposed its own definition of "national interest." Its government responded with varying success to diverse and mounting pressures, as it tried to intercept at the gate the flow of foreign capital and to control for its own benefit the effects of external economic forces upon which economic growth--and its own power--chiefly depended.

APPENDIX

THE INDIANS IN COLONIAL SPANISH AMERICA

by

Arlene Eisen

INTRODUCTION

The contradictions and weaknesses engendered by the Spanish bureaucratic-patrimonial system resulted in a fragmented system of authority. The Crown's failure to achieve unity becomes particularly visible vis-a-vis the situation of the Indians in colonial Spanish America. The Indians, who constituted the economic and social base of society, were, by their critical role in the colonial economy, a central point of controversy in the drive for wealth, which demanded the exploitation of an indigenous labor force, and the drive for expansion and unification of Spain's Christian empire. The latter involved paternal protection as well as conversion of a vast pagan population. The tension between economic necessities and Christian beliefs in part accounts for the Crown's inability to fully exploit the New World's resources. In addition, it frequently had to rely on disloyal groups to organize the labor force for the extraction of wealth.

This situation will become clearer as we analyze the means whereby Indians were incorporated into the colonial system. We shall see to what degree the Indians were vassals of the king and, alternatively, to what degree they were instruments of production to be exploited by elements whose own autonomy challenged the king's sovereignty. The economic exigencies of the colonial system led to the development of institutions which exploited the Indians despite royal attempts at protective legislation. Even where the evangelizing impulse was predominant, the institutions of tutelage were designed to pacify the Indians, and few channels were open for them to state their needs.

The discussion of the Indians and the colonial order which follows will focus mainly on developments in Peru. Before proceeding to the main body of the discussion, it will be useful to attempt a very brief sketch of Indian society in Peru before the arrival of Pizarro. After discussing various areas of tension (political, economic, and social) that developed as a result of the Conquest, we will analyze the character of Indian social movements and protests.

SPANISH BUREAUCRATIC-PATRIMONIALISM IN AMERICA

The accomplishments of the Inca dynasty of Peru have interested numerous historians and anthropologists and are well documented.[1] Ruling over sixteen million people inhabiting an immense territory from southern Colombia to the Maule River in Chile and from the Pacific Ocean to the Amazon jungles, the Inca dynasty controlled an empire that had become too large and heterogeneous to be governed effectively. (The Spaniards only hastened the disintegration process.)[2] The native populations ruled by the Incas were all incorporated in a highly ordered political and social system. Every level of society was hierarchically ordered and subordinate to the person of the absolute sovereign. No man held office except by authority, direct or delegated, of the Inca. Since there were no horizontal bonds linking officials of equal rank, to capture the supreme ruler was tantamount to capturing the empire. The population was largely sedentary, accustomed to living in towns, and trained to regular industry. It paid moderate tribute to the Inca in the form of produce or labor, which was used largely for public works. (Money was unknown.) The Inca's intricate paternal rule made life secure and stable, and the Incaicas' animistic-type religious system was relatively "advanced."

After the conquest by the Spaniards, the Incaicas were considered an organic part of colonial society. The Indian populations in other areas, however, such as southern Chile and La Plata, were not incorporated into the colonial system. In southern Chile, the few warrior Araucanians who survived the struggle against the Spanish existed on the periphery of society as slaves. In La Plata, where the Indians were not numerous but were warlike, they remained largely on the frontier of the colonial society rather than becoming constituent parts.

THE POLITICO-RELIGIOUS ADMINISTRATION OF THE INDIANS

The Spanish American colonies were organized on the premise that the King of Castile was the sole owner and arbiter of his possessions by the grace of the apostolic donation of Pope Alexander VI in the papal bulls of 1493.[3] Later we shall examine the non-metaphysical interpretations of this mandate, but first we must deal with the religious obligations the bulls imposed.

---

[1]See, for example, Philip A. Means, The Fall of the Inca Empire (New York: Scribners, 1932); Pedro de Cieza de Leon, The Incas (Norman, Okla.: University of Oklahoma Press, 1960); J. Alden Mason, The Ancient Civilization of Peru (Harmondsworth: Penguin Books, 1957).

[2]Means, op. cit., pp. 5-7.

[3]Ibid., p. 139.

APPENDIX: THE INDIANS IN COLONIAL SPANISH AMERICA

Although the concern for winning new adherents was a dominant factor in the Church's dealings with the many pagan vassals in the colonies, there was no single or monolithic ideology for dealing with the problems of Christian penetration in the New World.[4] Nor did enterprising missionaries follow a single pattern in drawing the largely reluctant Indians into the fold. Conversion took varying forms: naked coercion, bribery, cajolery, negotiation, or any combination thereof.

The most common technique for securing religious control over the heathens was the reading of the requerimiento. The theological basis for using the requerimiento was found in the thirteenth-century writings of the Cardinal Bishop of Ostia. There it was maintained that, according to natural law, "heathens had their own political jurisdiction and possessions before Christ. Upon Christ's arrival, all powers and the rights of dominion held by heathens passed to Christ, who became lord over the earth, both in the spiritual and temporal sense."[5] Of course this dominion was delegated to Christ's successors, St. Peter and the succeeding popes, and hence through the Patronato Real to the Catholic king. All conquistadors read the requerimiento (in Spanish) to the Indians, informing them that it was the right of Christ, through his representative the pope, to hold the infidel world in subjugation. Then, if the Indians did not submit themselves freely, they were considered in rebellion and could be legally and morally coerced into subjugation.

It is not surprising that most of the new converts were somewhat superficial Christians. Mariategui commented: "La evangelizacion de la America Espanola no puede ser enjuiciada como una empresa religiosa, sino como una empresa eclesiastica."[6] Even colonial authorities recognized the perfunctory nature of the conversions. In 1565, Governor Castro complained to the king that although some 300,000 Indians had been baptized, it would be difficult to find forty real Christians in their number.[7] The Crown's

---

[4]See Silvio Zavala, New Viewpoints on the Spanish Colonization of America (Philadelphia: University of Pennsylvania Press, 1943), pp. 29 ff., for varying religious attitudes toward the Indians. It is interesting to note in this context that the Inquisition provided no significant direct impetus to the evangelizing process.

[5]Ibid., pp. 6-7.

[6]Jose Carlos Mariategui, Siete ensayos de interpretacion de la realidad Peruana (6a. ed.; Lima: Amauta, 1958), p. 157. Translation: "The evangelization of Spanish America cannot be judged as a religious enterprise but only as an ecclesiastical enterprise."

[7]John Howland Rowe, "The Incas Under Spanish Colonial Institutions," Hispanic American Historical Review, May, 1957, p. 184.

reaction was somewhat less than perfunctory. When it was discovered that Indians were still practicing their traditional rites in secret, <u>visitadores de idolatria</u> were sent to end the heresy in the style of the Inquisitors of the times.

The local priest (<u>cura</u>) was the main keeper of the spiritual welfare of his Indian charges. Each Indian community of 200 had a <u>cura</u>, supported by the tribute the Indians paid. The <u>cura</u> was supposed to give instruction in reading and writing, as well as in the Christian doctrine. Although many exceptions have been documented, the clergy became better known for its abusive than for its protective treatment of the Indians. Few Indians were ordained until the late eighteenth century, and the majority of <u>curas</u> were Creoles and <u>mestizos</u>. The Cloth became a relatively lucrative calling for those excluded from the higher ranks of the colonial administration. Priests exacted illegal fees, unpaid personal services, and exorbitant "gifts" from the people (in collusion with local governmental officials).

However, it would be wrong to condemn the entire clergy for malpractice. There were members of the clergy who staunchly defended the Indians against the rapacity of <u>encomenderos</u> and <u>corregidores</u>. Protective legislation, however ineffective, was often stimulated by the persistent pleas of well-placed clergy. Many Indians sought refuge from forced labor in the burgeoning missions --in particular, Jesuit missions--which were known for the good life the Indians lived within their confines. But mission life brought absolute spiritual discipline that reduced the Indians to the state of docile children rather than "free vassals."

The evangelizing impulse had implications for secular as well as religious life. The papal bulls of 1493 lent themselves to the interpretation that Spanish monarchs were the political lords of the Indies.[8] While the Indians were declared free vassals of the Crown, their liberty was sharply limited by the Crown's tutelary orientation towards them, as well as the social and economic exigencies of the drive for wealth.

To make possible evangelization and collection of royal tribute, the Crown ordered the resettlement of scattered Indians into <u>reducciones</u>. Each <u>reduccion</u> (or village) had a church, school, and local form of government. But as with so many of the king's edicts, the order was not enforced until he had a strong representative in the colony. Viceroy Toledo (1562-1582) carried out the wholesale resettlement of more than a million-and-a-half Indians.[9] Toledo's reorganization of Indian society is said to

---

[8]Zavala, <u>op. cit.</u>, p. 24.

[9]Rowe, <u>op. cit.</u>, p. 156.

APPENDIX: THE INDIANS IN COLONIAL SPANISH AMERICA

mark the end of the Spanish Conquest.[10] He finally quelled Manco Inca's guerilla harassments in 1572 and destroyed the last recalcitrant Indian government, which had been in exile in Vilcabamba. However, although Toledo broke up old clan ties and tore the people away from their traditional shrines, much of Inca culture remained only superficially altered.

As in other spheres where the king's tutelary intentions were contravened by the local officials, the protective functions of the <u>reducciones</u> were commonly subverted. Each community, for instance, had a fund (<u>caja de comunidad</u>) accumulated from the produce of common lands or from labor. Its income was supposed to be used to defray municipal expenses such as legal services, support of the hospital, aid to widows, etc. Yet, typically, the funds were administered by <u>corregidores de Indios</u> who used them as private capital for their own business enterprises.[11]

The Crown, as sovereign protector of its vassals, held them to be minors in a perpetual state of tutelage. Indians could not bear arms, ride horses, consume wine, or hold dances without permission. (Later, we shall see how the two most important institutions in the administration of the Indians--the <u>mita</u> and the <u>encomienda</u>--though their establishment was motivated partially by the tutelary impulse, became the basic instruments of exploitation by autonomous elements.) Although intermarriage was tolerated so as to spread Christianity, the progeny of such intermarriages were barred from inheriting the posts of their <u>cacique</u> fathers. However, this tabu failed to prevent rampant collusion between <u>caciques</u> and local Creole officials, and the Crown could not counterbalance the growing power of the <u>corregidores</u>. (When the office of <u>cacique</u> was not inherited, it would often be filled by the <u>corregidor</u>'s choice from three viceregal nominees.)

However, as Professor Morse notes, as the Indian people were absorbed, they were not indiscriminately reduced to a common stratum.[12] The Spaniards encouraged survival of the native nobility, hoping to manipulate it. <u>Caciques</u> could bypass the <u>corregidor</u> and appeal directly to the king or his proxy, the viceroy, for redress of certain grievances. However, even those few who might be able to afford the journey to Lima found these officials emi-

---

[10]<u>Ibid</u>.

[11]C. H. Haring, <u>The Spanish Empire in America</u> (New York: Harcourt, Brace & World, 1963), p. 162.

[12]Richard M. Morse, "Political Theory and the Caudillo," in Hugh H. Hamill, ed., <u>Dictatorship in Spanish America</u> (New York: A. Knopf, 1965), p. 55.

SPANISH BUREAUCRATIC-PATRIMONIALISM IN AMERICA

nently unsympathetic to the Indians.

The traditional rank of cacique thus became part of the administrative hierarchy. Haring observes that those caciques who associated with Europeans quickly assimilated.[13] They were exempt from tribute payment and mita service, and had jurisdiction over minor criminal offenses. But their real function became the collection of tribute and mitayos. Therefore, to the extent that the mita and tribute were used to foster an autonomous Creole class, most caciques collaborated in the erosion of the Crown's control over colonial society. Ironically, however, in our discussion of Indian rebellions, we will find some caciques attempting to thwart their erstwhile collaborators in the name of the king.

THE SOCIO-ECONOMIC ADMINISTRATION OF THE INDIANS

The Crown's inability to exploit colonial wealth directly helped develop a relatively autonomous, economically powerful Creole group. The task of organizing the indigenous labor force fell largely into the hands of this Creole group. Their drive for wealth and prestige precluded concern for the welfare or tutelage of the Indian population. This Creole class grew in significance as the colonial order eroded. The fate of the New Laws of 1542 dramatically illustrates the process. Charles V's promulgation of the New Laws represented not only a response to Friar Casas' (the "Apostle of the Indians") proddings for more benevolent treatment of the Indians, but also an attempt by the king to consolidate his hold over the colonial economy. The powers and duties of the Council of the Indies, the audiencias, viceroys, oidores, etc., as direct representatives of the Crown, were detailed minutely.[14]

The audiencias were instructed to terminate all enslavement and abuse of Indians and their obligation to serve in dangerous employments. More importantly, the laws contained a formal declaration that Indians were free persons and protected vassals of the Crown, thereby prohibiting any form of involuntary servitude. All officials (lay and clerical) who held encomiendas or repartimientos were ordered to cede them to the Crown. All persons holding Indians without authorization likewise were to hand their labor force over to the Crown. A ceiling was placed on the number of encomiendas an individual could hold, and the excess was placed under the Crown's domain. No new encomiendas were to be granted, and those already in existence could not be inherited, but were to pass to the Crown. Encomiendas could be confiscated if Indians

---

[13]Haring, op. cit., p. 199.

[14]See Means, op. cit., pp. 84 ff., for details.

APPENDIX: THE INDIANS IN COLONIAL SPANISH AMERICA

were ill-treated, and protectors were appointed to execute this provision. Finally, any leader implicated in the factional strife between Pizarro and Almagro in Peru would lose his encomienda. Means notes that this last provision deprived practically every encomendero in Peru of his holdings, for the leaders in that strife had nearly all been of the encomendero class.[15]

Charles V appointed Don Blasco Núñez Vela as viceroy to execute the New Laws. The encomenderos desperately appealed to Gonzalo Pizarro to lead their resistance and take up arms against the king's betrayal of their interests. Markham observed that Pizarro's revolution owed much of its attraction to the "harshness and blunders of the Viceroy."[16] Means characterized the new viceroy as a "highborn cavalier who presently revealed himself to be the possessor of a mentality like that of a lunatic hyena."[17] Pizarro, with the approval of the oidores, wrote to the king pleading for revocation of the hated laws. Meanwhile, matters were brought to a head when the viceroy murdered a popular official in September, 1544. The oidores arrested Núñez Vela on fifty-nine charges and seized supreme command. A month later the oidores were terrorized into appointing Gonzalo Pizarro Governor and Captain-General to hold office until the king should order otherwise. The unfortunate viceroy escaped, but was later defeated in a bloody battle by Pizarro. There was pressure on the reluctant Pizarro to crown himself and create an independent feudal kingdom.

This separatist plan never materialized. The king revoked the New Laws in 1546, and Pizarro's cause was robbed of its momentum. Gasca, the shrewd new president of the audiencia, granted amnesty to the rebels and secured their loyalty to the Crown by granting large shares of Indians and lands. The internecine strife which continued was more a form of bickering over control of wealth than a secessionist movement.

However, there were new uprisings after 1552 under the command of Francisco Girón following an announcement that the mita would be abolished. Indeed, civil order was not restored until the rule of Toledo in 1569. His frequent "visitas" or personal inspections of trouble spots cowed many rebels. Toledo sacrificed reform at the altar of consolidation. The king, content with relative stability and increasing funds, no longer insisted on Indian protection.

---

[15]Ibid., p. 85.

[16]Sir Clements R. Markham, A History of Peru (Chicago: Siegel & Co., 1892), p. 122.

[17]Means, op. cit., p. 85.

SPANISH BUREAUCRATIC-PATRIMONIALISM IN AMERICA

Toledo's *Libro de Tasas*, promulgated in 1572, provided a political framework for the economic exploitation of the Indians. The most significant effect of these edicts was the entrenchment of the *corregidor*. The *corregimiento*, or administrative region, had been known in the colonies long before Toledo. Before 1540 the Crown had tried to use the *corregidores* to oppose the pretensions of the *encomenderos*.[18] But it was not until Toledo that the *corregimiento* became an administrative unit sufficiently important to provoke massive Indian rebellions. The institution was designed to serve several purposes. The *corregidor* would collect taxes from the natives for the king's coffers. At the same time, he was to protect the Indians from illegal exactions by priests, *encomenderos*, and local *caciques*. Finally, he was to determine the Indians' needs and provide for their material welfare.

A. The Corregimiento: An examination of the *corregidor*'s powers shows how his functions were quickly perverted.[19] Royal magistrate with power to act in all legal disputes, to punish all infractions of the law, and to put into execution all measures of "good government," he superseded all judicial officers within his jurisdiction and had power over all of them. To protect his charges from corruption, he was to ban all gambling, prevent usurious interest rates, and forbid any night shows or immoral plays. He kept the financial records of his territory. He could pass ordinances affecting local administration which had the same force as law. However, his economic functions were more important than his legislative and judicial powers. He not only had the monopoly of trade with the Indians in his district, but also regulated all prices on produce to be exported.

To check malpractice in government, no individual was permitted to hold the office of *corregidor* in the district in which he resided, nor might *encomenderos* or proprietors of lands and mines be appointed to that office within the area in which their property was located. The *corregidor*'s term was five years if he had been appointed in Spain by the king and three if he was named by the viceroy. There were the usual strict penalties for malfeasance.[20] Nevertheless, Haring remarks,

The multiplicity of regulations often repeated in Royal in-

---

[18]Zavala, *op. cit.*, p. 75.

[19]The following discussion of the *corregidor*'s powers is liberally adapted from C. E. Castaneda, "The Corregidor in Spanish Colonial Administration," *Hispanic American Historical Review*, November, 1929, pp. 453-66.

[20]Haring, *op. cit.*, pp. 129-30.

APPENDIX: THE INDIANS IN COLONIAL SPANISH AMERICA

structions and decrees, is sufficient evidence that honesty and integrity in provincial government were not easy to maintain. Removed from effective control of the Crown by the intervening ocean, protected from interference by the Viceroy and Audiencia, except for serious cause, corregidors and provincial governors, especially if they owed their appointment to the Crown, were in a position to exercise considerable independence and sometimes tyrannical authority.[21]

Thus, once again, we find the breakdown of the Crown's control. Characteristically, as Haring implies, the abuses were perpetrated by the elements upon which the Crown most heavily relied. When the banner of Indian rebellion was raised, as we shall see later, it was against the European *corregidores*. The paternal economic control the *corregidor* exercised preordained the most flagrant abuses, for it was only through abuse that the "zero-sum game" for wealth could be won. Armed with the exclusive right to trade with the Indians within their several districts, the *corregidores* would force Indians to buy goods useless to them at exorbitant prices.[22] This practice was called "*repartimiento* of goods," not to be confused with the "*repartimiento* of Indians." Indians worked for the *corregidor* for wages, but, in reality, were slaves, since their meager salaries were inadequate to pay tribute and debts. The *corregidor* also forced his charges to sell their produce to him at prices far below the market value to enlarge his profit. The list of abuses can easily be extended, but we shall not belabor the point here except to note that the principle of private appropriation underlay these abuses.

It is sufficient to note that the *corregimiento* became such a lucrative position that by the 1670's the systematic sale of *corregimientos* was well entrenched. Although the king could not destroy the power of the *corregidores*, by 1756 he attempted to curb the worst abuses. He formally recognized their power by legalizing the *repartimiento* of goods and then attempting to regulate prices. This edict, however, only exacerbated the deteriorating situation. The decree was interpreted as a royal license to steal. For example, tribute funds were credited to *repartimiento* payments, so that the king's name could be invoked in making collections, however brutal.[23]

---

[21] Ibid., p. 31.

[22] Markups averaged 400%. See Bernard Moses, *South America on the Eve of Emancipation* (New York: G. P. Putnam's Sons, 1908), p. 174.

[23] Rowe, op. cit., p. 167.

SPANISH BUREAUCRATIC-PATRIMONIALISM IN AMERICA

B. Indian Slavery: The political conception of Indians as free vassals of the king proved to be incompatible with the institution of slavery in its traditional form. The Crown could not very well control a labor force that was owned privately by other individuals. In addition, the enslavement of rebellious Indians captured in war was practiced long after the final decree to ban slavery was issued in 1548. Slavery was at its worst in frontier regions where there was no stable, dense nuclei of Indian people on which to build Spanish institutions. While the enslavement of prisoners never took on great significance in Peru, the Chilean landlords depended more and more upon the natives captured in the interminable wars against the Araucanians, as the number of free Indians sharply diminished owing to frequent epidemics, brutality, and heavy labor in the gold mines.[24] The Rio de la Plata's frontier pattern resembled the Chilean practice with regard to slavery.[25]

C. The Mita: The most general manner in which labor was organized was the repartimiento de indios, later adapted in Peru under the name "mita." Repartimiento de indios referred to the allotment of Indians for necessary tasks in the Spanish community, such as building, mining, agriculture, and transportation. (Encomienda, or allotment of Indians to a specific individual, implied a repartimiento, but not all repartimientos were encomiendas.) Work was compulsory, and until 1609, unpaid. Haring suggests that the mita and the repartimiento were always considered by the authorities in Spain to be makeshift, with the hope that they would ultimately be supplanted by free labor (or Negro slavery).[26]

With the abolishment of compulsory labor tribute and the unpaid repartimiento, the Crown had hoped to foster the development

---

[24]Haring, op. cit., p. 63.

[25]On the other hand, Negro enslavement persisted until Independence. In areas where the Indian labor force was scarce, the exploiter depended on Negro slaves. Also, only Negroes were permitted to work in the sugar mills and other miscellaneous private enterprises. By this restriction the Crown attempted to limit the areas of control by autonomous elements. While human imports from Africa were significant in other areas of the Indies, they were never brought to Peru on a large scale.

[26]Op. cit., p. 62. Although exact figures on the proportion of free and mita labor are unavailable, we may safely assume that the mita was the predominant mode of employment among the Indians. And perhaps, we may account for the Crown's desultory regulation of the mita's abuses by noting that the Crown never considered it a permanent institution.

APPENDIX: THE INDIANS IN COLONIAL SPANISH AMERICA

of a free, voluntary labor force. However, after their initial work experience under the Spanish masters, it is not difficult to understand why the Indians did not come rushing to work as free laborers. The Indians' reluctance to work, combined with the rapacity of Spaniards and Creoles, provided a fertile climate for the development of a convenient rationale for coercion. The Indian was regarded as "lazy" and, given the colonizer's tutelary responsibilities, he had to be forced to work for his "own good."

Under the *mita* system, Indians of different regions lived freely under the same tutelage. However, their liberty was limited by their *mita* service. All household heads (*haturuna*) were obligated to work a given number of days per year at a specific task. For example, they would be paid for fifteen days' domestic service, three or four months' pastoral duty, ten months' work in the mines, etc. Those who tilled the king's apportioned lands, craftsmen (*yanaconas*),* and *caciques* were exempt.[27] The *mitayo* was not excused from paying the regular tribute assessment; moreover, his wages were never as high as those paid to native laborers on the free market.

Toledo ruled that one-seventh (and at times of labor shortage, one-fifth) of the *haturunas* must serve as *mitayos* at a time. But the steady shrinkage of the Indian population rendered the *mita* far more onerous than Toledo had expected.[28] *Caciques* administered the drawing of lots for the *mita* upon request of the *corregidor*. The *mita de plaza* was the most common form. *Mitayos* would be corralled in the plaza and hired out for construction, farm, and general service. Their pay was barely enough for food, and at times they had to travel up to ten days without pay to the workplace. The *mita* also provided labor for the *obrajes* (cloth factories), *chasquis* (post running), *huacas* (forced digging for old Inca treasures in the tombs), pearl fishing, cocoa tending, lumber cutting, transport, etc.

However, the mines were the major wealth-producing enterprise in Peru, and *mitayos* took on their greatest economic significance as workers in the silver and mercury mines. Rowe insists that the *mita* system remained the basis of Peruvian mining until

---

*<u>Yanaconas</u>, under the Inca rule, had been indentured servants, but under the Spanish masters, they became a relatively privileged independent laboring class.

[27] Jose Ots Capdequi, <u>Instituciones sociales de la America espanola en el periodo colonial</u> (Buenos Aires: La Plata, 1934), p. 22.

[28] Means, <u>op. cit.</u>, p. 164.

SPANISH BUREAUCRATIC-PATRIMONIALISM IN AMERICA

the end of the colonial period.[29] On the other hand, Haring notes that in the eighteenth century the practice spread of commuting personal service of the mita for money payment made by the cacique or corregidor responsible for supplying the labor quota. The corregidor preferred to keep the Indians at home for his own use, and the miner used the payment for hired labor which was generally more efficient.[30] The miners evidently found the constant shifting of mita Indians less profitable than skilled permanent labor (probably composed of detribalized Indians).

We find evidence to support Haring's thesis in two other aspects of the labor situation. Zavala notes that miners manipulated their "free" workers' indebtedness so as to make slavery the reality of the free labor force.[31] Secondly, mitayos in the mines sharply declined in absolute terms. According to Markham, the mita in Potosi produced 11,199 laborers in 1573, and a hundred years later, though conscription was not relaxed, there were only 1674 mitayos.[32] Forced labor separated men from their wives, but probably depopulation may be attributed more to the barbaric abuses the mitayos suffered than to these separations. Under the continuous work system, for instance, Indians were kept underground for six consecutive days and severely punished when they did not fulfill their quotas.[33]

---

[29]Op. cit., p. 172.

[30]Op. cit., p. 66.

[31]Op. cit., p. 101.

[32]Op. cit., p. 193. Moses' statistics sharply differ with Markham's, although they point to the same enormous depopulation. Moses claims that 4/5 of the mitayos died within their first year of service ["Flush Times in Potosi," Papers on the Southern Spanish Colonies in America (Berkeley: University of California Press), pp. 6-7]. The mercury mines were not any more healthful than the mines in Potosi. Two-thirds of the Indians who worked in Huancavelica died in the mercury mines (Means, op. cit., p. 181).

[33]Some detail of the onerous mita system serves to emphasize the Crown's failure to control the violent, wealth-accumulating classes. Indians were forced to wear their hair long to facilitate their capture and transport to various work sites. Conditions in the cloth factories were so infamous that condemned Indians were sent to the obrajes as punishment. Workers were locked in the factories for 16 hours and severely whipped when quotas were not fulfilled. Kidnapping for mita service was rampant, and when all male adults had been dragged off, only women and children were left to till the fields. Boys only six years old labored in the

APPENDIX: THE INDIANS IN COLONIAL SPANISH AMERICA

The chief sources of royal revenue, that is, the tribute paid by the Indians and one-fifth of all mining produce, depended on Indian labor. Therefore, as long as a viceroy substantially added to the royal treasury, the Crown would tolerate deviance from its edicts. We see then how Toledo effectively contravened the king's orders when he obliged the Indians to cease paying tribute in produce and pay it in silver instead. His purpose--to induce Indians to work in the silver mines--greatly served the interests of the wealthy miners.

Of course the Crown attempted protection of its vassals to counterbalance the growing audacity of the Creoles. Toledo, the great consolidator, for example, appointed Indian protectors in every considerable community. Typically, however, the appointees were too frequently changed. They lacked sufficient personal prestige to withstand the wealthy landowners and miners or to carry influence with the judges, and they did little but collect salaries and betray the confidence reposed in them by the Indians.[34]

Protective laws inevitably feel into disuse in the hands of the corregidores. Laws regulating hours, pay, travel, and conscription were left to local officials to enforce, and there is no reason to believe that the corregidor was any more diligent in executing mita regulation than he was in performing any other of the Crown's trusts.

D. The Encomienda: The encomienda "was the most important economic base for the new aristocracy."[35] About half of the Indian population lived in encomiendas.[36] The encomienda served a dual function: to reward the conquerors in service and tribute, and to incorporate the Indians into Christian civilization. In fact, the encomienda represented the most direct example of the contradictions and weaknesses inhering in Spanish bureaucratic-patrimonial systems.

The encomienda was a concession, conferred ultimately by

---

obrajes, and wages were withheld while they were forced into debt slavery. Tribute was exacted from villages, not individuals, so that when the population decreased, the same sum burdened the increasingly desperate inhabitants who remained.

[34]Haring, op. cit., p. 56.

[35]Ots Capdequi, op. cit., p. 25.

[36]Means, op. cit., p. 154. He estimates that another fourth lived in Indian towns established by the Crown, and that the last fourth lived in independent Indian communes.

royal favor, of a number of Indians to a preferred Spaniard. The grantee assumed the obligation of instructing the Indians in the Catholic faith and defending them. In return, the Indians were obliged to pay their protector a tribute in money, kind, and/or personal service. The Capitulación of 1529, the Crown's enabling order for Pizarro to conquer Peru, granted Pizarro the right to confer encomiendas. During the following two decades there were no restrictions on tribute or service levies. By 1561, available statistics suggest that a significantly large encomendero class had emerged. There were 427 encomienda villages, of which only fifty belonged to the Crown or were unassigned.[37]

However powerful the encomenderos became by the seventeenth century, it is important to note that their grants did not convey land rights.[38] Cabildos granted land (mercedes de tierras), and after the defeat of the Armada, the Crown freely sold lands to restore the Spanish treasury. Also, Indians commonly abandoned their land to the Spaniards and fled to other provinces, since outsiders (forasteros) were exempt from mita and tribute obligations until 1732. Only the governor or viceroy granted titulos de encomienda. The size of the grant was determined by the number of Indians composing it, and the grant might apply to lands held by Indians, Crown lands, lands acquired by the encomendero through a grant distinct from his title as encomendero, or lands belonging to other Spaniards. However, the encomendero was legally forbidden to own land on the encomienda and to live in the territory longer than was necessary to collect tribute taxes. Thus, Zavala suggests that the encomienda could not have been the direct precursor of the modern hacienda, since the former did not involve true ownership of lands.[39]

---

[37]Sergio Bagú, Estructura social de la colonia (Buenos Aires: Ateneo, 1952), p. 90.

[38]Although the Crown vacillated in allowing inheritance of encomiendas by law, in fact succession was nearly automatic. The civil wars in response to the New Laws, which would have ended the institution through attrition, proved to the king that in order to make the colonies profitable he would have to accommodate the encomenderos.

[39]Zavala, op. cit., p. 83. In Amerique Latine (Paris: Presse Universitaires de France, 1963), pp. 79 ff., Jacques Lambert maintains, contrary to Zavala and F. A. Kirkpatrick ("The Landless Encomienda," Hispanic American Historical Review, XXII, 4, November, 1942, pp. 765-74) that the latifundia evolved directly from the encomienda. While encomenderos often became latifundistas, it was their wealth, rather than their defunct titles to Indians, that facilitated this transition.

APPENDIX: THE INDIANS IN COLONIAL SPANISH AMERICA

In addition to denying land rights, the Crown made further attempts to curb the rise of a feudal encomendero class to rival his power. Politically he tried to substitute for the particularistic system of feudal estates a centralized monarchical system administered by transient governors who were required to return frequently to Spain to ensure their loyalty to the central government. The laws regarding encomiendas also reflected this political aim. In our treatment of the New Laws, we have already seen how the Crown ventured to limit succession and inheritance of encomiendas. Moreover, members of the Council of the Indies, viceroys, presidents, oidores, alcaldes de crimen, fiscales, contadores de cuentas, oficiales reales, governors, and their close relatives were barred from holding encomiendas. Separation of powers legally prevailed down to the local level--that is, the corregidor or alcalde mayor, not the encomendero, administered justice.

The Crown also issued positive prescriptions which, had they been enforced, would have sharply limited the encomenderos' economic power. In keeping with the evangelizing impulse, we find many royal orders for the protection of Indians in encomiendas. Tribute might be levied only upon men between the ages of 18 and 50. And while the encomendero was to personally supervise the Indians' spiritual and temporal welfare, visitadores surveyed districts for injustices, and audiencias heard complaints on behalf of the Indians. The Crown obliged the encomendero to provide for a priest for the Indians under his jurisdiction, and, at times, these priests defended their flock against excessive abuses.[40]

The Crown had no choice but to depend on the encomenderos to organize the labor force to exploit the colonial riches. As one Dominican wrote: "[T]here could be no permanence in the land without rich men, or rich men without encomiendas, because all industry was carried on by Indian labor, and only those having Indians were able to carry on commerce."[41] Although the Crown never sought "permanence in the land" by an autonomous aristocracy, the Crown did demand wealth and could not create it without men seeking riches. The Crown unwittingly created the basis for a

---

[40] The myriad of protective edicts attests to the rampant abuses of the Indians. Indians could not be sold or lent, forced to carry unreasonable burdens, employed at times when they planted their own crops, transported out of their own districts, etc. Nevertheless, economic and political exigencies weighed against protection of Indians and control of encomendero power. In Chile, for instance, restrictive legislation was ignored in favor of securing the support of the encomenderos in the war against the Araucanians.

[41] Quoted in Haring, op. cit., p. 53.

feudal aristocracy by favoring discoverers, conquerors, and settlers ("civilizers") with encomiendas.

We can now discuss the decline of the encomienda. First, we must remember the fantastic decline of the Indian population. As the Indian disappeared, so did the encomienda. The process was most rapid in Chile. In 1656 there were 102 encomiendas of ten or more Indians in Santiago alone. In 1749 there were less than fifty encomiendas in all of Chile, including those with less than ten Indians.[42] This decline, owing mostly to the extinction of the Indian population, facilitated Governor Ambrosio O'Higgins' final suppression of the remaining encomiendas in 1790.

In Peru the explanation for the decline of the encomienda is more complicated. Gradually, the encomienda became a less and less desirable privilege, as the king's portion of the tribute increased and the ban on personal service was enforced. The Crown became more rigorous in collecting encomienda tribute as the treasury at home became depleted, and, in turn, the encomenderos became less rigorous in their opposition to restrictions as they found more wealth in the growing industry and commerce. As the Crown took over forfeited encomiendas, royal holdings became enormous, and the king ordered their sale. Thus private landowning gradually superseded encomiendas. Finally, in 1718, all encomiendas began to revert to the Crown upon the death of the owner.

In spite of the disappearance of the encomienda, however, the lot of the Indian did not improve. The abuses of the corregidor and mita persisted, and various rules maintained the Indian in his inferior social and economic position. For instance, in an Edict of 1706 the audiencia of Lima ordered that no Indian (or Negro, zambo, or mulatto) could conduct trade or commerce, own a store, or even sell produce in the streets.[43]

THE INDIAN REACTION

After Toledo finally subdued Manco Inca's guerrilla harassments late in the sixteenth century, a situation of relative calm prevailed for over a hundred years. After that, while plots or rebellions were all abortive, there was growing discontent among exploited groups. We can classify such revolts on the basis of their goals. At one end of a continuum we place purely Indianist revolts attempting to restore the Inca monarchy. Second, we find separatist attempts with no clearly defined ideology. Third, there were solely reformist protests and revolts. Finally, there

---

[42]Kirkpatrick, op. cit., p. 772.

[43]Bagú, op. cit., p. 135.

APPENDIX: THE INDIANS IN COLONIAL SPANISH AMERICA

were amorphous harassment tactics.

AIMS OF INDIAN PROTESTS AND REBELLIONS[44]

Restore Inca Monarchy	Independence	Reformist	Harassment
1737: Under Belez de Cordoba in S. Peru & Bolivian Altoplano (in name of pope) 1739: Plot discovered in Oruro	1666-67: Under Gabriel Manco Capac in Lima, factionalized and betrayed 1742-56: Under Cacique Juan Santos Atahualpa, in Montana and Sierra 1750: In Lima, plot to crown Santos betrayed	1664: Cacique Collatopa (Cajamarca), nonviolent protest to king against corregidores and doctrineros 1722-32: Cacique Mora Chimo Capac presented four grievance memorials to Court in Madrid 1749: Inca nationalists in Lima sent envoys to Spain with memorials addressed to king and pope 1765: Quito rebellion under "Don Juan" against abuses, bad government, and taxes, not king 1780: Cochabamba rebellion under the banner "Viba el Rey, muera el mal gobierno"[45]	1737-38: Large scale attack in 17 provinces in Azangoro

---

[44]Sources: Boleslao Lewin, La Rebelion de Tupac Amaru (Buenos Aires: Libreria Hachette, 1957), esp. pp. 118 ff.; Rowe, op. cit., pp. 57-58; Coronel Jose A. Vallejo, La Rebelion de 1742 Juan Santos (Lima: El Primer Congreso Nacional de Historia, 1954).

[45]Translation: "Long live the king; death to the evil government."

SPANISH BUREAUCRATIC-PATRIMONIALISM IN AMERICA

From the above table the overwhelming reformist nature of manifest Indian protests is evident, and the predominant role of cacique leadership. Evidently those caciques who were not co-opted by corrupt local officials had a rather naive faith in the structures the Crown had erected for the protection of the Indians. Peaceful protests were invariably ignored; violent ones were either betrayed before they erupted or pitilessly suppressed.

Rebellion of Tupac Amaru: Scholars, although they debate the real goals of Tupac Amaru in his rebellion of 1780-1781, concur in characterizing the rebellion as the most significant Indian uprising in colonial history. The Spanish authorities were not unaware of the Indian discontent. We may cite Visitador Areche, the man who ruthlessly crushed the rebellion, who, despite his cruelty, could aptly characterize the ailments of colonial society: "The lack of righteous judges, the mitas of the Indians and provincial commerce of the corregidors have made a corpse of this America, . . . [T]he corregidors are interested only in themselves . . ."[46] However, Areche's severe fiscal policy to increase the Crown's treasury, which only exacerbated the steadily deteriorating situation, illustrates the inability of the Crown's representatives to mediate conflicting aims successfully.

Morse suggests that Indians and Negroes, unlike the medieval serf, never fully identified with the historical and cultural ethos of their masters, thereby encouraging a more exploitative psychology.[47] Rowe supports this contention by noting that the caciques had a special incentive to maintain and transmit Inca cultural traditions, since their title to office was based on the fact that an ancestor belonged to Inca nobility.[48] Thus, the Crown promoted a culture apart from the Spanish order by perpetuating the traditional Inca chiefs. At the same time, this policy made exploitation, from elements external to the Indian tradition, inevitable.

When we are reminded that most protests were made in the name of the king for the protection of his vassals, we may infer that that part of the cultural ethos which the Indians might have internalized was most difficult to realize in the face of the exploitation to which they were in fact subjected. The connection with the king that they defended was not mediated by the interven-

---

[46] Areche's letter of 1780 to Spain, quoted in Eunice Joiner Gates, "Don Jose Antonio de Areche: His Own Defense," Hispanic American Historical Review, February, 1928, p. 22.

[47] Op. cit., p. 57.

[48] Op. cit., p. 157.

APPENDIX: THE INDIANS IN COLONIAL SPANISH AMERICA

ing hierarchy. In other words, the king's paternalistic preoccupation with his "free vassals" was contradicted in reality by the king's agents who, whether for their own profit or for the economic benefit of the Crown, considered the Indians as "factors of production." Reduced by violence, the Indians in turn resorted to violence to assert their political and social linkage with the Spanish order, once their peaceful appeals to "their lord" proved to be in vain.

The *cacique* Tupac Amaru II began negotiations and complaints to the *audiencia* in Lima as early as 1770. (The violent revolt did not begin until ten years later, with Tupac's kidnapping and the assassination of the oppressive *corregidor* of Tinta. Even after this initial violence, Tupac proceeded with military campaigns only after exhausting peaceful petitions in Cuzco.) The demands made by Tupac Amaru included the following: abolition of the *mita* and *repartimientos*; abolition of the *corregidores*; abolition of *obrajes*, monopoly stores, and other customs and taxes that burdened the Indians; expulsion of the *chapetones* (European-born Spaniards) who held the *corregimientos*; appointment of *alcaldes mayores* in each province to administer justice; establishment of an *audiencia* in Cuzco more accessible to the Indians than the one in Lima. Acevedo adds that there is some evidence that Tupac also aimed for the appointment of Inca descendants as viceroys.[49] He also made an appeal for the liberation of all Negro slaves. With this appeal, Tupac hoped to stimulate slave risings under his banner and emphasize the humanitarian nature of his demands.

It is interesting to note that although Tupac Amaru declared war without quarter on the European-born Spaniards, his demands did not mention anything about the agricultural *haciendas* established by so many *chapetones* by taking Indian land. Nor did Tupac ever make a single pronouncement against the Catholic religion, the Church or the clergy, probably not so much to win the clergy to his cause, but rather not to alienate religious Indians and Creoles.

Tupac addressed his demands to the Crown and higher representatives in the name of the Crown. He did not challenge the king's right to rule over the colony. Before attacking Cuzco with his 60,000 men, Tupac addressed letters to the *cabildo* and municipality. He prefaced his demands to the *cabildo* with the following: "As heir of the Incas he was stimulated to end abuses and see men appointed to govern who would respect the laws of the King of Spain." To the Bishop of Cuzco he wrote that he came forth on behalf of the whole nation to put an end to the outrages of the

---

[49] Edberto Oscar Acevedo, *La Rebelion de Tupac Amaru* (Buenos Aires: Mendoza, 1958), pp. 21-22.

SPANISH BUREAUCRATIC-PATRIMONIALISM IN AMERICA

corregidores, and he promised to respect all priests, the church property, women, and inoffensive unarmed people.[50] One contemporary wrote: "Tupac Amaru es el mas distinguido campeon de Su Majestad; la fidelidad es su principal virtud."[51]

To secure Indian support for his rebellion, Tupac Amaru utilized Indianism, its corollary--xenophobia--and the Indian's material desperation. Tupac's establishing his claim to the Inca lineage was probably his first political act. Born in 1742, he was baptised Jose Gabriel Condorcanqui, and succeeded his father as cacique of Tinta twenty years later in 1770. When Charles III, through the audiencia in Lima, granted him the title Marquis de Oropesa, he adopted the name Tupac Amaru II.[52]

His title served a dual purpose. It legitimized his role as leader of the Indian masses and strengthened his influence with the Spaniards. He made a special point of cultivating the friendship of Spanish officials, hoping thereby to persuade them to improve the miserable conditions of the Indians. He took advantage of the title he owed to Charles III by beginning all his letters and pronouncements, "Tengo ordenes reales . . . ."[53] At the same time he revived dormant Indian pride and cohesion around the old Inca title. Tupac became a symbol of past glory and the possibility for regaining it.

A rallying point was found in hostility to European-born Spaniards. The chapeton was a symbol of oppression visible to the masses as a monopolizer of all significant sources of power. Unfortunately, statistics showing the percentage of Creole corregidores, encomenderos, etc., are unavailable. However, it was the Creoles who represented the growing economic power, and the Indian rebels misplaced their hostility. Tupac sought allies among the Creoles, even though the latter always remained suspicious of Indian cooperation and made their protests separately.

---

[50]Markham, op. cit., p. 201.

[51]Quoted in Daniel Valcarcel, La Rebelion de Tupac Amaru (Mexico: Fondo de Cultural Economica, 1947), p. 180. Translation: "Tupac Amaru is the most distinguished champion of His Majesty; loyalty is his principal virtue." [My translation.]

[52]According to Means, in "The Rebellion of Tupac Amaru II," Hispanic American Historical Review, February, 1919, Jose Gabriel Condorcanqui was the grandson of Tupac Amaru I, son of Manco Inca.

[53]Lewin, op. cit., p. 400. Translation: "I have royal orders to . . ." [My translation.]

APPENDIX: THE INDIANS IN COLONIAL SPANISH AMERICA

From the church steps of every village, arrayed in full Inca regalia, Tupac addressed the people in the Quechua language, proclaiming that he came to abolish economic abuses and punish corregidores. (No wonder they proclaimed him their redeemer.) He capitalized on popular hatred for the corregidores to the fullest extent. Tupac reinforced his case by proclaiming the mita abolished.

The kidnapping of Aliaga, the corregidor of Tinta, and his execution in the presence of a large crowd of Indians was the signal for a general uprising. As he issued the execution order Tupac asserted, "Esta orden no es contra Dios, ni contra el Rey, sino contra las malas introducciones."[54] With the money, muskets (75), horses, and mules that Tupac had compelled Aliaga to sign over, the rebel leader was able to win new recruits. His first victory at Sangarara encouraged more Indians to join his ranks and then proceed to destroy and pillage obrajes and stores of the local corregimientos.

The rebellion spread at a remarkable rate. All except 20 caciques of Peru (and there were over 2,000) declared themselves in favor of Tupac Amaru. We have already noted that his military ranks exceeded 60,000. Some caciques, however, di remain loyal to the Spaniards; 700 fought against Tupac in Sangarara. (To appreciate the significance of this figure, we may point out that the Argentino-Chilean army of San Martin in the Peruvian campaign had only 4,414 men.)[55] Uprisings broke out simultaneously in many parts of the viceroyalty in Peru and even Argentina.

The reactions of Spaniards and Creoles to the rebellion not only reflected the tensions within the colonial order, but they foreshadowed Creole-Indian relationships during the Independence movement. The severity of the suppression of the rebellion radicalized the Indian movement.[56] The Spaniards demanded nothing short of unconditional defeat of the rebels. Visitador Areche, who far eclipsed the viceroy at the time, went to Cuzco with extraordinary powers and a well-armed army of 15,000. Tupac Amaru offered to negotiate his demands without more bloodshed, but Areche refused all negotiations and arrogantly wrote to Tupac that, if

---

[54] Ibid., p. 420. Translation: "This is not an order against God, nor against the king, but against the evil new practices."

[55] Ibid., p. 438.

[56] See Markham, Lewin, et al. Since there is no conclusive evidence that the rebellion of Tupac Amaru ever became a separatist movement, we cannot fully support this hypothesis, however logical it seems.

he surrendered at once, the mode of his execution would be less cruel. It was at this point, maintains Markham, that Tupac became convinced that the solution could be only independence or death.[57]

Tupac Amaru was defeated in the spring of 1781. Public tortures preceded infamous executions by quarterization. Areche succeeded in exterminating the Inca dynasty completely by murdering over 80,000 within the next year. Inca and *cacique* dress was banned, and all pictures of Incas destroyed. Presentations of Quechua dramas were banned, and Indian musical instruments burned. All signs of mourning were severely punished, and the Quechua language forbidden. (The fact that today approximately 70 percent of the Peruvian population still speak Quechua and don Indian dress attests to the ineffectiveness of these orders.)

Perhaps the harshness of the reprisals may be attributed to the *visitador*'s surety that the rebellion was actively supported by the Creoles. Spanish authorities assumed that Creole discontent and Indian desperation thoroughly united the two groups. We need only quote Areche to indicate the Spanish anxiety over the possibility of a generalized revolt. In his report of the execution he wrote, "They hurled satires and insults at my officials and attendants; they did not wish the rebellion to be of Indians alone because of the extortion of the corregidors, but also of the mestizos and of all the kingdom because of customs and new taxes."[58]

Exactly how sympathetic to the rebellion were the Creoles? We know that the Creoles evolved into a gentry without political power, deeply resentful of the Spaniards. They were consistently excluded from higher colonial offices and treated with disdain by pretentious low-born Spaniards. Growing Creole discontent is reflected in the sizable number of Creole separatist conspiracies of the eighteenth century.[59] It is not surprising then that Tupac Amaru should seek Creole support. However, the divergence of Creole and Indian motivations for revolt precluded any effective cooperation between the two groups. Indian rebellions were too menacing to the Creoles to be integrated into the latter's own revolts. The rebellion of Tupac Amaru only served to highlight the potential danger to Creole economic hegemony that the Indians presented.

Even Lewin, who claims that the Creoles were sympathetic

---

[57]Markham, *op. cit.*, p. 203; also Moses, *op. cit.*, p. 206.

[58]Quoted in Gates, *op. cit.*, p. 29.

[59]See Lewin's chapter on this subject for details. *Op. cit.*, pp. 114 ff.

APPENDIX: THE INDIANS IN COLONIAL SPANISH AMERICA

with the Indian uprising, admits that no proof exists of ties between Tupac and subversive Creole movements of the era.[60] Nor is there evidence that the Jesuits or other clergymen aided the Indian movement, except as isolated individuals. The Creole uprising of Oruro in 1781 perhaps best illustrates the hesitancy of the Creoles to throw their lot in with the Indians. The mines had been faring poorly, and no credit was available to the Creole miners. They finally revolted against the Spaniards, the *corregidor* fled, and a rich Creole miner was declared chief of Oruro by the rebels. The Indians aided the Creole rebels; however, the Creoles soon turned against their allies. In the end, when bribery failed, the Creoles expelled the militant Indians from the town and began collaboration once again with the Spaniards.

The "most significant rebellion" in pre-Independence times was sharply limited by the reformist ideology of the leadership and lack of Creole support. Even if we assume that Tupac Amaru ultimately aimed for independence, his vacillation in accomplishing the task cost him victory. Hoping to secure reforms, he hesitated in attacking Cuzco just long enough to allow the Spaniards to strengthen their forces. However, he could only have had faith in reform if he accepted the conception of the Indians as "free vassals"--a notion that precluded a thrust for independence.[61]

The name of Tupac Amaru became a symbol of the possibility for future revolts and has often been invoked by various rebels for innumerable causes. The Indians were defeated, but they were by no means placated. The cruelty of the Spanish reaction encouraged them to join the Creoles in later rebellions (only to be disappointed with their new legal overlords).

---

[60] Ibid., pp. 402-4.

[61] Late in the 1780's *corregidores* were replaced by *intendentes* and an *audiencia* was established in Cuzco. However, these reforms, stimulated partly by the rebellion, brought little improvement.

GLOSSARY OF SPANISH TERMS

Acordada: Established by royal decree in 1710 in New Spain, it was "a revival of the . . . rura constabulary first created in the middle of the sixteenth century for the pursuit and summary punishment of brigands in the country districts. . . . [T]he tribunal employed a force of some 2500 agents, most of whom rendered service without pay for the honor and privileges it conferred on them in their own communities . . ." (Haring).

Adelantado: Castilian distinction bestowed on the conquistadors of the first phase of the colonization, "it carried with it the governorship of the territory subdued, with proprietary rights, which also was often transmissible by inheritance to a second generation" (Haring).

Alcalde: Magistrate. (1) Alcalde ordinario: leading magistrate of a cabildo, chosen by the regidores or councilors. (2) Alcalde del crimen: member of the criminal chamber of an audiencia. (3) Alcalde mayor: district officer comparable to a corregidor.

Asesor: Assessor.

Audiencia: A high judicial court endowed also with legislative and administrative powers, such as reviewing the acts of the viceroy or, in general, the president of the audiencia.

Audiencia Praetorial: The audiencia seated in the capital of the viceroyalty. In administrative matters it functioned much like a council of state to the viceroy.

Bandeira: Armed band of early explorers in Brazil.

Cabildo: Town council. Composed of regidores and alcaldes ordinarios, plus other municipal officers, such as the alferez real (herald or municipal standard bearer), alguacil mayor (chief constable), depositario general (public trustee), fiel ejecutor (inspector of weights and measures, charged with the supply of foodstuffs and the adjustment of market prices), and receptor de penas (collector of judicial fines).

Cabildo abierto: "An extraordinary assembly called together only at long intervals (or in an emergency) and only those citizens who were especially invited had the right to attend" (Haring).

Cacique: Indian chief.

Captain-General: High executive office, originally equivalent to

GLOSSARY

commander-in-chief. The captain-general "exercised supreme authority within his jurisdiction as the direct representative of the King" (Haring). Where there was a viceroy, the viceroy exercised the functions of captain-general.

Casa de Contratación: Board of Trade, the agency which administered economic relations between Spain and her colonies, located at Seville.

Caudillo: A political boss with a military following loyal to him personally.

Cedula: Decree.

Chacra: Farm.

Chapeton: Nickname given by Creoles to peninsular Spaniards.

Consulado: The exclusive guild of merchants originally formed in Seville. "As a kind of chamber of commerce it possessed administrative authority in matters concerning trade and communications" (Haring).

Contador: Accountant and auditor in the colonial exchequer.

Corregidor: Provincial officer with administrative and judicial authority, subordinate to the viceroy or captain-general and to the audiencia of his district.

Corregimiento: The district and/or office of a corregidor.

Cortes: Parliamentary assembly.

Doctrinero: Curate in charge of Indian parishes.

Encomienda: "The patronage conferred by royal favor over a portion of the natives concentrated in settlements near those of the Spaniards; the obligation to instruct them in the Christian religion . . . and to defend them in their persons and property; coupled with the right to demand tribute or labor in return for these privileges. So far as we know, no grant of land was involved" (Haring). Sometimes used interchangeably with the word repartimiento.

Encomendero: The recipient of an encomienda.

Estancia: Estate (applies in particular to Argentine cattle estates).

Fiscal: Prosecuting attorney in an audiencia.

GLOSSARY

Fueros: Privileges or charter rights of a regional or corporate character. More generally: specific rights.

Gobernador: An officer of higher rank than the provincial officers such as the *corregidores* or *alcaldes mayores*. He sometimes held the title of captain-general. "The district [he] administered . . . was usually of greater territorial extent than the *corregimiento* or the *alcaldia mayor*, and its territory was less definitely associated with a single town than was the case in the other administrative units" (Haring).

Gamonal: Local *caudillo* or party boss (Peru).

Hacendado: The owner of a *hacienda*.

Hacienda: Landed property or estate. Also means public finances.

Hidalguía: Title of nobility. Also the rights of an *hidalgo*, among which was the right to be called *Don*.

Huaso: Chilean cowboy or peasant (in a pejorative sense). Equivalent to the Argentine *gaucho*.

Intendente: The eighteenth-century official who replaced governors and *corregidores*. The head of a province or intendancy (eighteenth-century administrative divisions). Full title: *Gobernador Intendente*.

Junta: Committe or board (applied to the revolutionary committees after 1810).

Junta Superior de Real Hacienda: Special board of finance to the highest executive in the province.

Juzgado de Indios: A special court established in the 1570's in New Spain and thirty years later in Peru which handled the judicial affairs concerning suits between Indians or between Indians and Spaniards.

Mayorazgo: The right of entailing an estate in favor of the firstborn son. Also his right of primogeniture.

Mesta: Corporation of sheep raisers.

Mita: The periodical conscription of Indians for manual work (Peru). "In the eighteenth century the practice spread of commuting personal service of the *mita* for a money payment made by the *curaca* (or *cacique*) or by the *corregidor* responsible for supplying the labor quota" (Haring).

Mitayo: An Indian working under the *mita* system.

GLOSSARY

Obraje: Cloth factory.

Oficiales Reales de Hacienda: Offices of the exchequer.

Oidor: Magistrate of an audiencia.

Patriarch of the Indies: "[A]s vicar-general [he] was presumed to have general superintendence of all ecclesiastical matters in the New World, and to reside at the Court so that he might be in immediate contact with the Council of the Indies. He generally bore the title and honors belonging to the cardinalate, and served at the same time as chief chaplain of the royal palace. But his functions appear to have remained largely honorary, and to have had little part in the government of the Church in America" (Haring). The first Patriarch was named in 1513.

Presidencia: The district over which a given audiencia had jurisdiction.

Procurador: Solicitor, procurator (generally a municipal function).

Protomedicato: Special administrative court regulating the medical profession.

Real Cuerpo de Mineria: Mining guild composed of a central tribunal in Mexico and provincial courts in each mining district.

Recurso de Fuerza: "Appeal to secular justice against abuse of authority by an ecclesiastical judge, as when he claimed jurisdiction not belonging to him or tried to prevent lawful appeals" (Haring).

Reducciones: Communities similar to Indian reservations in North America.

Regent (of the audiencia): Post established in 1776. "An official who ranked next below the viceroy or captain-general and presided over the chamber of justice in his absence" (Haring).

Regidor: Councilor in a cabildo.

Regimiento: The office of a regidor.

Repartimiento: See Encomienda.

Requerimiento: A proclamation read to the Indians by a notary of the conquistador demanding their allegiance to the pope and the King of Castile.

Residencia: "Judicial review of an official's conduct at the end of his term of office" (Haring).

GLOSSARY

Sub-delegado: Subordinate of the <u>intendente</u> for an administrative subdivision of the intendancy.

Superintendente: After the administrative reforms of the eighteenth century, "an official independent of the viceroy, in charge of economic and financial affairs. . . . Under this arrangement the viceroy and audiencia were shorn of virtually all their fiscal attributes. But the division of authority immediately proved to be impracticable, and within a few years the two offices of viceroy and superintendent general were combined in the same person" (Haring).

Teniente: Lieutenant of a <u>corregidor</u>.

Tesorero: Treasurer.

Vecino: The owner of a house in a town. When the towns were founded, land was distributed among the first dwellers or <u>vecinos</u>. The status also conferred municipal rights. Not all the inhabitants of a town were <u>vecinos</u>.

Visita: Ordinary (or exceptional) inspection of a whole viceroyalty or captaincy-general (conducted by a <u>visitador-general</u>) or of a particular province or official (conducted by a <u>visitador</u>). The <u>visitadores</u> were directly appointed by the king and the Council of the Indies. The viceroy or president, in consultation with the <u>audiencia</u>, also appointed commissioners for local <u>visitas</u> of <u>corregidores</u> or other minor officials.